Terence Rattigan

Born in 1911, a scholar at Harrow and at Trinity College, Oxford,
Terence Rattigan had his first long-running hit in the West End
at the age of twenty-five: *French Without Tears* (1936). His next
play, *After the Dance* (1939), opened to euphoric reviews yet
closed under the gathering clouds of war, but with *Flare Path*
(1942) Rattigan embarked on an almost unbroken series of
successes, with most plays running in the West End for at least a
year and several making the transition to Broadway: *While the Sun
Shines* (1943), *Love in Idleness* (1944), *The Winslow Boy* (1946),
The Browning Version (performed in double-bill with
Harlequinade, 1948), *Who is Sylvia?* (1950), *The Deep Blue Sea*
(1952), *The Sleeping Prince* (1953) and *Separate Tables* (1954).
From the mid-fifties, with the advent of the 'Angry Young Men', he
enjoyed less success on stage, though *Ross* (1960) and *In Praise of
Love* (1973) were well received. As well as seeing many of his
plays turned into successful films, Rattigan wrote a number of
original plays for television from the fifties onwards. He was
knighted in 1971 and died in 1977.

Terence Rattigan

THE WINSLOW BOY

Introduced by
Dan Rebellato

NICK HERN BOOKS

London
www.nickhernbooks.co.uk

A Nick Hern Book

This edition of *The Winslow Boy* first published in Great Britain
in 1994 by Nick Hern Books, The Glasshouse, 49a Goldhawk
Road, London W12 8QP. *The Winslow Boy* was included in Volume
One of *The Collected Plays of Terence Rattigan* published in 1953
by Hamish Hamilton

Reprinted 1999, 2002, 2004, 2006, 2009, 2011, 2012

Copyright © Trustees of the Terence Rattigan Trust 1953
Introduction copyright © Dan Rebellato 1994
Front cover photo copyright © Hulton Deutsch Collection

Typeset by Country Setting, Kingsdown, Deal, Kent
Printed and bound in Great Britain by Mimeo Ltd, Huntingdon,
Cambridgeshire PE29 6XX

A CIP catalogue record for this book is available from
the British Library

ISBN 978 1 85459 467 9

Woodland
CARBON
www.woodlandcarbon.co.uk
NICK HERN BOOKS
Printed on Carbon Captured paper

Terence Rattigan (1911-1977)

Terence Rattigan stood on the steps of the Royal Court Theatre, on 8 May 1956, after the opening night of John Osborne's *Look Back in Anger*. Asked by a reporter what he thought of the play, he replied, with an uncharacteristic lack of discretion, that it should have been retitled 'Look how unlike Terence Rattigan I'm being.' [1] And he was right. The great shifts in British theatre, marked by Osborne's famous première, ushered in kinds of playwriting which were specifically unlike Rattigan's work. The pre-eminence of playwriting as a formal craft, the subtle tracing of the emotional lives of the middle classes – those techniques which Rattigan so perfected – fell dramatically out of favour, creating a veil of prejudice through which his work even now struggles to be seen.

Terence Mervyn Rattigan was born on 10 June 1911, a wet Saturday a few days before George V's coronation. His father, Frank, was in the diplomatic corps and Terry's parents were often posted abroad, leaving him to be raised by his paternal grandmother. Frank Rattigan was a geographically and emotionally distant man, who pursued a string of little-disguised affairs throughout his marriage. Rattigan would later draw on these memories when he created Mark St Neots, the bourgeois Casanova of *Who is Sylvia?* Rattigan was much closer to his mother, Vera Rattigan, and they remained close friends until her death in 1971.

Rattigan's parents were not great theatregoers, but Frank Rattigan's brother had married a Gaiety Girl, causing a minor family uproar, and an apocryphal story suggests that the 'indulgent aunt' reported as taking the young Rattigan to the theatre may have been this scandalous relation.[2] And when, in the summer of 1922, his family went to stay in the country cottage of the drama critic Hubert Griffiths, Rattigan avidly worked through his extensive library of playscripts. Terry went to Harrow in 1925, and there maintained both his somewhat illicit theatregoing habit and his insatiable reading, reputedly devouring every play in the school library. Apart from contemporary authors like Galsworthy, Shaw and Barrie, he also read the plays of Chekhov, a writer whose crucial influence he often acknowledged.[3]

His early attempts at writing, while giving little sign of his later sophistication, do indicate his ability to absorb and reproduce his own theatrical experiences. There was a ten-minute melodrama about the Borgias entitled *The Parchment*, on the cover of which the author recommends with admirable conviction that a suitable cast for this work might comprise 'Godfrey Tearle, Gladys Cooper, Marie Tempest, Matheson Lang, Isobel Elsom, Henry Ainley . . . [and] Noël Coward'.[4] At Harrow, when one of his teachers demanded a French playlet for a composition exercise, Rattigan, undaunted by his linguistic shortcomings, produced a full-throated tragedy of deception, passion and revenge which included the immortal curtain line: 'COMTESSE. (*Souffrant terriblement*.) Non! non! non! Ah non! Mon Dieu, non!'[5] His teacher's now famous response was 'French execrable: theatre sense first class'.[6] A year later, aged fifteen, he wrote *The Pure in Heart,* a rather more substantial play showing a family being pulled apart by a son's crime and the father's desire to maintain his reputation. Rattigan's ambitions were plainly indicated on the title pages, each of which announced the author to be 'the famous playwrite and author T. M. Rattigan.'[7]

Frank Rattigan was less than keen on having a 'playwrite' for a son and was greatly relieved when in 1930, paving the way for a life as a diplomat, Rattigan gained a scholarship to read History at Trinity, Oxford. But Rattigan's interests were entirely elsewhere. A burgeoning political conscience that had led him to oppose the compulsory Officer Training Corps parades at Harrow saw him voice pacifist and socialist arguments at college, even supporting the controversial Oxford Union motion 'This House will in no circumstances fight for its King and Country' in February 1933. The rise of Hitler (which he briefly saw close at hand when he spent some weeks in the Black Forest in July 1933) and the outbreak of the Spanish Civil War saw his radical leanings deepen and intensify. Rattigan never lost his political compassion. After the war he drifted towards the Liberal Party, but he always insisted that he had never voted Conservative, despite the later conception of him as a Tory playwright of the establishment.[8]

Away from the troubled atmosphere of his family, Rattigan began to gain in confidence as the contours of his ambitions and his identity moved more sharply into focus. He soon took advantage of the university's theatrical facilities and traditions. He joined The Oxford Union Dramatic Society (OUDS), where contemporaries included Giles Playfair, George Devine, Peter Glenville, Angus Wilson and Frith Banbury. Each year, OUDS ran a one-act play competition and in Autumn 1931 Rattigan submitted one. Unusually, it seems that this was a highly experimental effort, somewhat like Konstantin's piece in *The Seagull*. George Devine, the OUDS president, apparently told the young author, 'Some of it is absolutely smashing, but it goes too far'.[9] Rattigan was instead to make his first mark as a somewhat scornful reviewer for the student newspaper, *Cherwell*, and as a performer in the Smokers (OUDS's private revue club), where he adopted the persona and dress of 'Lady Diana Coutigan', a drag performance which allowed him to discuss leading members of the Society with a barbed camp wit.[10]

That the name of his Smokers persona echoed the contemporary phrase, 'queer as a coot', indicates Rattigan's new-found confidence in his homosexuality. In February 1932, Rattigan played a tiny part in the OUDS production of *Romeo and Juliet*, which was directed by John Gielgud and starred Peggy Ashcroft and Edith Evans (women undergraduates were not admitted to OUDS, and professional actresses were often recruited). Rattigan's failure to deliver his one line correctly raised an increasingly embarrassing laugh every night (an episode which he re-uses to great effect in *Harlequinade*). However, out of this production came a friendship with Gielgud and his partner, John Perry. Through them, Rattigan was introduced to theatrical and homosexual circles, where his youthful 'school captain' looks were much admired.

A growing confidence in his sexuality and in his writing led to his first major play. In 1931, he shared rooms with a contemporary of his, Philip Heimann, who was having an affair with Irina Basilevich, a mature student. Rattigan's own feelings for Heimann completed an eternal triangle that formed the basis of the play he co-wrote with Heimann, *First Episode*. This play was accepted for production in Surrey's "Q" theatre; it was respectfully received and subsequently transferred to the Comedy Theatre in London's West End, though carefully shorn of its homosexual subplot. Despite receiving only £50 from this production (and having put £200 into it), Rattigan immediately dropped out of college to become a full-time writer.

Frank Rattigan was displeased by this move, but made a deal with his son. He would give him an allowance of £200 a year for two years and let him live at home to write; if at the end of that period, he had had no discernible success, he would enter a more secure and respectable profession. With this looming deadline, Rattigan wrote quickly. *Black Forest*, an O'Neill-inspired play based on his experiences in Germany in 1933, is one of the three that have survived. Rather unwillingly, he collaborated with Hector Bolitho on an adaptation of the latter's novel, *Grey Farm*, which received a disastrous New York production in 1940. Another project was an adaptation of *A Tale of Two Cities*, written with Gielgud; this fell through at the last minute when Donald Albery, the play's potential producer, received a complaint from actor-manager John Martin-Harvey who was beginning a farewell tour of his own adaptation, *The Only Way*, which he had been performing for forty-five years. As minor compensation, Albery invited Rattigan to send him any other new scripts. Rattigan sent him a play provisionally titled *Gone Away*, based on his experiences in a French language Summer School in 1931. Albery took out a nine-month option on it, but no production appeared.

By mid-1936, Rattigan was despairing. His father had secured him a job with Warner Brothers as an in-house screenwriter, which was reasonably paid; but Rattigan wanted success in the theatre, and his desk-bound life at Teddington Studios seemed unlikely to advance this ambition. By chance, one of Albery's productions was unexpectedly losing money, and the wisest course of action seemed to be to pull the show and replace it with something cheap. Since *Gone Away* required a relatively small cast and only one set, Albery quickly arranged for a production. Harold French, the play's director, had only one qualm: the title. Rattigan suggested *French Without Tears*, which was immediately adopted.

After an appalling dress rehearsal, no one anticipated the rapturous response of the first-night audience, led by Cicely Courtneidge's infectious laugh. The following morning Kay Hammond, the show's female lead, discovered Rattigan surrounded by the next day's reviews. 'But I don't believe it', he said. 'Even *The Times* likes it.' [11]

French Without Tears played over 1000 performances in its three-year run and Rattigan was soon earning £100 a week. He moved out of his father's home, wriggled out of his Warner Brothers contract, and dedicated himself to spending the money as soon as it came in. Partly this was an attempt to defer the moment when he had to follow up this enormous success. In the event, both of his next plays were undermined by the outbreak of war.

After the Dance, an altogether more bleak indictment of the Bright Young Things' failure to engage with the iniquities and miseries of contemporary life, opened, in June 1939, to euphoric reviews; but only a month later the European crisis was darkening the national mood and audiences began to dwindle. The play was pulled in August after only sixty performances. *Follow My Leader* was a satirical farce closely based on the rise of Hitler, co-written with an Oxford contemporary, Tony Goldschmidt (writing as Anthony Maurice in case anyone thought he was German). It suffered an alternative fate. Banned from production in 1938, owing to the Foreign Office's belief that 'the production of this play at this time would not be in the best interests of the country',[12] it finally received its première in 1940, by which time Rattigan and Goldschmidt's mild satire failed to capture the real fears that the war was unleashing in the country.

Rattigan's insecurity about writing now deepened. An interest in Freud, dating back to his Harrow days, encouraged him to visit a psychiatrist that he had known while at Oxford, Dr Keith Newman. Newman exerted a svengali-like influence on Rattigan and persuaded the pacifist playwright to join the RAF as a means of curing his writer's block. Oddly, this unorthodox treatment seemed to have some effect; by 1941, Rattigan was writing again. On one dramatic sea crossing, an engine failed, and with everyone forced

to jettison all excess baggage and possessions, Rattigan threw the
hard covers and blank pages from the notebook containing his new
play, stuffing the precious manuscript into his jacket.

Rattigan drew on his RAF experiences to write a new play, *Flare
Path*. Bronson Albery and Bill Linnit who had both supported
French Without Tears both turned the play down, believing that
the last thing that the public wanted was a play about the war.[13]
H. M. Tennent Ltd., led by the elegant Hugh 'Binkie' Beaumont,
was the third management offered the script; and in 1942, *Flare
Path* opened in London, eventually playing almost 700
performances. Meticulously interweaving the stories of three
couples against the backdrop of wartime uncertainty, Rattigan
found himself 'commended, if not exactly as a professional
playwright, at least as a promising apprentice who had definitely
begun to learn the rudiments of his job'.[14] Beaumont, already on
the way to becoming the most powerful and successful West End
producer of the era, was an influential ally for Rattigan. There is a
curious side-story to this production; Dr Keith Newman decided
to watch 250 performances of this play and write up the insights
that his 'serial attendance' had afforded him. George Bernard
Shaw remarked that such playgoing behaviour 'would have driven
me mad; and I am not sure that [Newman] came out of it without
a slight derangement'. Shaw's caution was wise.[15] In late 1945,
Newman went insane and eventually died in a psychiatric
hospital.

Meanwhile, Rattigan had achieved two more successes; the witty
farce, *While the Sun Shines*, and the more serious, though
politically clumsy, *Love in Idleness* (retitled *O Mistress Mine* in
America). He had also co-written a number of successful films,
including *The Day Will Dawn, Uncensored, The Way to the Stars*
and an adaptation of *French Without Tears*. By the end of 1944,
Rattigan had three plays running in the West End, a record only
beaten by Somerset Maugham's four in 1908.

Love in Idleness was dedicated to Henry 'Chips' Channon, the
Tory MP who had become Rattigan's lover. Channon's otherwise
gossipy diaries record their meeting very discreetly: 'I dined with
Juliet Duff in her little flat . . . also there, Sibyl Colefax and
Master Terence Rattigan, and we sparkled over the Burgundy. I
like Rattigan enormously, and feel a new friendship has begun. He
has a flat in Albany'.[16] Tom Driberg's rather less discreet account
fleshes out the story: Channon's 'seduction of the playwright was
almost like the wooing of Danaë by Zeus – every day the
playwright found, delivered to his door, a splendid present – a case
of champagne, a huge pot of caviar, a Cartier cigarette-box in two
kinds of gold . . . In the end, of course, he gave in, saying
apologetically to his friends, "How can one *not?*" '.[17] It was a very
different set in which Rattigan now moved, one that was wealthy
and conservative, the very people he had criticised in *After the*

Dance. Rattigan did not share the complacency of many of his friends, and his next play revealed a deepening complexity and ambition.

For a long time, Rattigan had nurtured a desire to become respected as a serious writer; the commercial success of *French Without Tears* had, however, sustained the public image of Rattigan as a wealthy young light comedy writer-about-town. [18] With *The Winslow Boy*, which premièred in 1946, Rattigan began to turn this image around. In doing so he entered a new phase as a playwright. As one contemporary critic observed, this play 'put him at once into the class of the serious and distinguished writer'.[19] The play, based on the Archer-Shee case in which a family attempted to sue the Admiralty for a false accusation of theft against their son, featured some of Rattigan's most elegantly crafted and subtle characterization yet. The famous second curtain, when the barrister Robert Morton subjects Ronnie Winslow to a vicious interrogation before announcing that 'The boy is plainly innocent. I accept the brief', brought a joyous standing ovation on the first night. No less impressive is the subtle handling of the concept of 'justice' and 'rights' through the play of ironies which pits Morton's liberal complacency against Catherine Winslow's feminist convictions.

Two years later, Rattigan's *Playbill*, comprising the one-act plays *The Browning Version* and *Harlequinade*, showed an ever deepening talent. The latter is a witty satire of the kind of touring theatre encouraged by the new Committee for the Encouragement of Music and Arts (CEMA, the immediate forerunner of the Arts Council). But the former's depiction of a failed, repressed Classics teacher evinced an ability to choreograph emotional subtleties on stage that outstripped anything Rattigan had yet demonstrated.

Adventure Story, which in 1949 followed hard on the heels of *Playbill*, was less successful. An attempt to dramatize the emotional dilemmas of Alexander the Great, Rattigan seemed unable to escape the vernacular of his own circle, and the epic scheme of the play sat oddly with Alexander's more prosaic concerns.

Rattigan's response to both the critical bludgeoning of this play and the distinctly luke-warm reception of *Playbill* on Broadway was to write a somewhat extravagant article for the *New Statesman*. 'Concerning the Play of Ideas' was a desire to defend the place of 'character' against those who would insist on the pre-eminence in drama of ideas.[20] The essay is not clear and is couched in such teasing terms that it is at first difficult to see why it should have secured such a fervent response. James Bridie, Benn Levy, Peter Ustinov, Sean O'Casey, Ted Willis, Christopher Fry and finally George Bernard Shaw all weighed in to support or condemn the article. Finally Rattigan replied in slightly more moderate terms to these criticisms insisting (and the first essay reasonably supports this) that he was not calling for the end of ideas in the theatre, but rather for their inflection through character and situation.[21] However, the damage was done (as, two years later, with his 'Aunt Edna', it would again be done). Rattigan was increasingly being seen as the arch-proponent of commercial vacuity.[22]

The play Rattigan had running at the time added weight to his opponents' charge. Originally planned as a dark comedy, *Who is Sylvia?* became a rather more frivolous thing both in the writing and the playing. Rattled by the failure of *Adventure Story*, and superstitiously aware that the new play was opening at the Criterion, where fourteen years before *French Without Tears* had been so successful, Rattigan and everyone involved in the production had steered it towards light farce and obliterated the residual seriousness of the original conceit.

Rattigan had ended his affair with Henry Channon and taken up with Kenneth Morgan, a young actor who had appeared in *Follow My Leader* and the film of *French Without Tears*. However, the relationship had not lasted and Morgan had for a while been seeing someone else. Rattigan's distress was compounded one day in February 1949, when he received a message that Morgan had killed himself. Although horrified, Rattigan soon began to conceive an idea for a play. Initially it was to have concerned a homosexual relationship, but Beaumont, his producer, persuaded him to change the relationship to a heterosexual one.[23] At a time when the Lord Chamberlain refused to allow any plays to be staged that featured homosexuality, such a proposition would have been a commercial impossibility. The result is one of the finest examples of Rattigan's craft. The story of Hester Collyer, trapped in a relationship with a man incapable of returning her love, and her transition from attempted suicide to groping, uncertain self-determination is handled with extraordinary economy, precision and power. The depths of despair and desire that Rattigan plumbs have made *The Deep Blue Sea* one of his most popular and moving pieces.

1953 saw Rattigan's romantic comedy *The Sleeping Prince*, planned as a modest, if belated, contribution to the Coronation festivities. However, the project was hypertrophied by the insistent presence of Laurence Olivier and Vivien Leigh in the cast and the critics were disturbed to see such whimsy from the author of *The Deep Blue Sea*.

Two weeks after its opening, the first two volumes of Rattigan's *Collected Plays* were published. The preface to the second volume introduced one of Rattigan's best-known, and most notorious creations: Aunt Edna. 'Let us invent,' he writes, 'a character, a nice respectable, middle-class, middle-aged, maiden lady, with time on her hands and the money to help her pass it'.[24] Rattigan paints a picture of this eternal theatregoer, whose bewildered disdain for modernism ('Picasso—"those dreadful reds, my dear, and why three noses?" ')[25] make up part of the particular challenge of dramatic writing. The intertwined commercial and cultural pressures that the audience brings with it exert considerable force on the playwright's work.

Rattigan's creation brought considerable scorn upon his head. But Rattigan is neither patronizing nor genuflecting towards Aunt Edna. The whole essay is aimed at demonstrating the crucial rôle of the audience in the theatrical experience. Rattigan's own sense of theatre was *learned* as a member of the audience, and he refuses to distance himself from this woman: 'despite my already self-acknowledged creative ambitions I did not in the least feel myself a being apart. If my neighbours gasped with fear for the heroine when she was confronted with a fate worse than death, I gasped with them'.[26] But equally, he sees his job as a writer to engage in a gentle tug-of-war with the audience's expectations: 'although Aunt Edna must never be made mock of, or bored, or befuddled, she must equally not be wooed, or pandered to or cosseted'.[27] The complicated relation between satisfying and surprising this figure may seem contradictory, but as Rattigan notes, 'Aunt Edna herself is indeed a highly contradictory character'.[28]

But Rattigan's argument, as in the 'Play of Ideas' debate before it, was taken to imply an insipid pandering to the unchallenging expectations of his audience. Aunt Edna dogged his career from that moment on and she became such a by-word for what theatre should *not* be that in 1960, the Questors Theatre, Ealing, could title a triple-bill of Absurdist plays, 'Not For Aunt Edna'.[29]

Rattigan's next play did help to restore his reputation as a serious dramatist. *Separate Tables* was another double-bill, set in a small Bournemouth hotel. The first play develops Rattigan's familiar themes of sexual longing and humiliation while the second pits a man found guilty of interfering with women in a local cinema against the self-appointed moral jurors in the hotel. The evening was highly acclaimed and the subsequent Broadway production a rare American success.

However, Rattigan's reign as the leading British playwright was about to be brought to an abrupt end. In a car from Stratford to London, early in 1956, Rattigan spent two and a half hours informing his Oxford contemporary George Devine why the new play he had discovered would not work in the theatre. When Devine persisted, Rattigan answered 'Then I know nothing about plays'. To which Devine replied, 'You know everything about plays, but you don't know a fucking thing about *Look Back in Anger*.'[30] Rattigan only barely attended the first night. He and Hugh Beaumont wanted to leave at the interval until the critic T. C. Worsley persuaded them to stay.[31]

The support for the English Stage Company's initiative was soon overwhelming. Osborne's play was acclaimed by the influential critics Kenneth Tynan and Harold Hobson, and the production was revived frequently at the Court, soon standing as the banner under which that disparate band of men (and women), the Angry Young Men, would assemble. Like many of his contemporaries, Rattigan decried the new movements, Beckett and Ionesco's turn from Naturalism, the wild invective of Osborne, the passionate socialism of Wesker, the increasing influence of Brecht. His opposition to them was perhaps intemperate, but he knew what was at stake: 'I may be prejudiced, but I'm pretty sure it won't survive,' he said in 1960, 'I'm prejudiced because if it *does* survive, I know I won't.' [32]

Such was the power and influence of the new movement that Rattigan almost immediately seemed old-fashioned. And from now on, his plays began to receive an almost automatic panning. His first play since *Separate Tables* (1954) was *Variation on a Theme* (1958). But between those dates the critical mood had changed. To make matters worse, there was the widely publicized story that nineteen year-old Shelagh Delaney had written the successful *A Taste of Honey* in two weeks after having seen *Variation on a Theme* and deciding that she could do better. A more sinister aspect of the response was the increasingly open accusation that Rattigan was dishonestly concealing a covert homosexual play within an apparently heterosexual one. The two champions of Osborne's play, Tynan and Hobson, were joined by Gerard Fay in the *Manchester Guardian* and Alan Brien in the *Spectator* to ask 'Are Things What They Seem?' [33]

When he is not being attacked for smuggling furtively homosexual themes into apparently straight plays, Rattigan is also criticized for lacking the courage to 'come clean' about his sexuality, both in his life and in his writing.[34] But neither of these criticisms really hit the mark. On the one hand, it is rather disingenuous to suggest that Rattigan should have 'come out'. The 1950s were a difficult time for homosexual men. The flight to the Soviet Union of Burgess and Maclean in 1951 sparked off a major witch-hunt against homosexuals, especially those in prominent positions. Cecil Beaton and Benjamin Britten were rumoured to be targets.[35] The police greatly stepped up the investigation and entrapment of homosexuals and prosecutions rose dramatically at the end of the forties, reaching a peak in 1953-54. One of their most infamous arrests for importuning, in October 1953, was that of John Gielgud.[36]

But neither is it quite correct to imply that somehow Rattigan's plays are *really* homosexual. This would be to misunderstand the way that homosexuality figured in the forties and early fifties. Wartime London saw a considerable expansion in the number of pubs and bars where homosexual men (and women) could meet. This network sustained a highly sophisticated system of gestural and dress codes, words and phrases that could be used to indicate one's sexual desires, many of them drawn from theatrical slang. But the illegality of any homosexual activity ensured that these codes could never become *too* explicit, *too* clear. Homosexuality, then, was explored and experienced through a series of semi-hidden, semi-open codes of behaviour; the image of the iceberg, with the greater part of its bulk submerged beneath the surface, was frequently employed.[37] And this image is, of course, one of the metaphors often used to describe Rattigan's own playwriting.

Reaction came in the form of a widespread paranoia about the apparent increase in homosexuality. The fifties saw a major drive to seek out, understand, and often 'cure' homosexuality. The impetus of these investigations was to bring the unspeakable and underground activities of, famously, 'Evil Men' into the open, to make it fully visible. The Wolfenden Report of 1957 was, without doubt, a certain kind of liberalizing document in its recommendation that consensual sex between adult men in private be legalized. However the other side of its effect is to reinstate the integrity of those boundaries – private/public, hidden/exposed, homosexual/heterosexual – which homosexuality was broaching. The criticisms of Rattigan are precisely part of this same desire to divide, clarify and expose.

Many of Rattigan's plays were originally written with explicit homosexual characters (*French Without Tears*, *The Deep Blue Sea* and *Separate Tables*, for example), which he then changed.[38] But many more of them hint at homosexual experiences and activities: the relationship between Tony and David in *First Episode*, the Major in *Follow my Leader* who is blackmailed over an incident in Baghdad ('After all,' he explains, 'a chap's only human, and it was a deuced hot night –'),[39] the suspiciously polymorphous servicemen of *While the Sun Shines*, Alexander the Great and T. E. Lawrence from *Adventure Story* and *Ross*, Mr Miller in *The Deep Blue Sea* and several others. Furthermore, rumours of Rattigan's own bachelor life circulated fairly widely. As indicated above, Rattigan always placed great trust in the audiences of his plays, and it was the audience which had to decode and reinterpret these plays. His plays cannot be judged by the criterion of 'honesty' and 'explicitness' that obsessed a generation after Osborne. They are plays which negotiate sexual desire through structures of hint, implications and metaphor. As David Rudkin has suggested, 'the craftsmanship of which we hear so much loose talk seems to me to arise from deep psychological necessity, a drive to organize the energy that arises out of his own pain. Not to batten it down but to invest it with some expressive clarity that speaks immediately to people, yet keeps itself hidden'.[40]

The shifts in the dominant view of both homosexuality and
the theatre that took place in the fifties account for the brutal
decline of Rattigan's career. He continued writing, and while
Ross (1960) was reasonably well received, his ill-judged musical
adaptation of *French Without Tears*, *Joie de Vivre* (1960), was
a complete disaster, not assisted by a liberal bout of laryngitis
among the cast, and the unexpected insanity of the pianist.[41] It
ran for four performances.

During the sixties, Rattigan was himself dogged with ill-health:
pneumonia and hepatitis were followed by leukaemia. When his
death conspicuously failed to transpire, this last diagnosis was
admitted to be incorrect. Despite this, he continued to write,
producing the successful television play *Heart to Heart* in 1962,
and the stage play *Man and Boy* the following year, which received
the same sniping that greeted *Variation on a Theme*. In 1964, he
wrote *Nelson – a Portrait in Miniature* for Associated Television,
as part of a short season of his plays.

It was at this point that Rattigan decided to leave Britain and live
abroad. Partly this decision was taken for reasons of health; but
partly Rattigan just seemed no longer to be welcome. Ironically, it
was the same charge being levelled at Rattigan that he had faced in
the thirties, when the newspapers thundered against the those who
had supported the Oxford Union's pacifist motion as 'woolly-
minded Communists, practical jokers and sexual indeterminates'.[42]
As he confessed in an interview late in his life, 'Overnight almost,
we were told we were old-fashioned and effete and corrupt and
finished, and . . . I somehow accepted Tynan's verdict and went off
to Hollywood to write film scripts'.[43] In 1967 he moved to
Bermuda as a tax exile. A stage adaptation of his Nelson play, as
Bequest to the Nation, had a luke-warm reception.

Rattigan had a bad sixties, but his seventies seemed to indicate a
turnaround in his fortunes and reputation. At the end of 1970, a
successful production of *The Winslow Boy* was the first of ten years
of acclaimed revivals. In 1972, Hampstead Theatre revived *While
the Sun Shines* and a year later the Young Vic was praised for its
French Without Tears. In 1976 and 1977 *The Browning Version* was
revived at the King's Head and *Separate Tables* at the Apollo.
Rattigan briefly returned to Britain in 1971, pulled partly by his
renewed fortune and partly by the fact that he was given a
knighthood in the New Year's honours list. Another double bill
followed in 1973: *In Praise of Love* comprised the weak *Before
Dawn* and the moving tale of emotional concealment and creativity,
After Lydia. Critical reception was more respectful than usual,
although the throwaway farce of the first play detracted from the
quality of the second.

Cause Célèbre, commissioned by BBC Radio and others,
concerned the Rattenbury case, in which Alma Rattenbury's aged

husband was beaten to death by her eighteen year-old lover. Shortly after its radio première, Rattigan was diagnosed with bone cancer. Rattigan's response, having been through the false leukaemia scare in the early sixties, was to greet the news with unruffled elegance, welcoming the opportunity to 'work harder and indulge myself more'.[44] The hard work included a play about the Asquith family and a stage adaptation of *Cause Célèbre*, but, as production difficulties began to arise over the latter, the Asquith play slipped out of Rattigan's grasp. Although very ill, he returned to Britain, and on 4 July 1977, he was taken by limousine from his hospital bed to Her Majesty's Theatre, where he watched his last ever première. A fortnight later he had a car drive him around the West End where two of his plays were then running before boarding the plane for the last time. On 30 November 1977, in Bermuda, he died.

As Michael Billington's perceptive obituary noted, 'his whole work is a sustained assault on English middle class values: fear of emotional commitment, terror in the face of passion, apprehension about sex'.[45] In death, Rattigan began once again to be seen as someone critically opposed to the values with which he had so long been associated, a writer dramatizing dark moments of bleak compassion and aching desire.

Notes.

1. Quoted in Rattigan's *Daily Telegraph* obituary (1 December 1977).

2. Michael Darlow and Gillian Hodson. *Terence Rattigan: The Man and His Work*. London and New York: Quartet Books, 1979, p. 26.

3. See, for example, Sheridan Morley. 'Terence Rattigan at 65.' *The Times*. (9 May 1977).

4. Terence Rattigan. Preface. *The Collected Plays of Terence Rattigan: Volume Two*. London: Hamish Hamilton, 1953, p. xv.

5. *Ibid.,* p. viii.

6. *Ibid.,* p. vii.

7. *Ibid.,* p. vii.

8. cf. Sheridan Morley, *op. cit.*

9. Humphrey Carpenter. *OUDS: A Centenary History of the Oxford University Dramatic Society*. With a Prologue by Robert Robinson. Oxford: Oxford University Press, 1985, p. 123.

10. Rattigan may well have reprised this later in life. John Osborne, in his autobiography, recalls a friend showing him a picture of Rattigan performing in an RAF drag show: 'He showed me a photograph of himself with Rattigan, dressed in a *tutu*, carrying a wand, accompanied by a line of aircraftsmen, during which Terry had sung his own show-stopper, "I'm just about the oldest fairy in the business. I'm quite the oldest fairy that you've ever seen".' John Osborne. *A Better Class of Person: An Autobiography, Volume I 1929-1956*. London: Faber and Faber, 1981, p. 223.

11. Darlow and Hodson *op. cit.*, p. 83.

12. Norman Gwatkin. Letter to Gilbert Miller, 28 July 1938. in: *Follow My Leader*. Lord Chamberlain's Correspondence: LR 1938. [British Library].

13. Richard Huggett. *Binkie Beaumont: Eminence Grise of the West Theatre 1933-1973*. London: Hodder & Stoughton, 1989, p. 308.

14. Terence Rattigan. Preface. *The Collected Plays of Terence Rattigan: Volume One*. London: Hamish Hamilton, 1953, p. xiv.

15. George Bernard Shaw, in: Keith Newman. *Two Hundred and Fifty Times I Saw a Play: or, Authors, Actors and Audiences*. With the facsimile of a comment by Bernard Shaw. Oxford: Pelagos Press, 1944, p. 2.

16. Henry Channon. *Chips: The Diaries of Sir Henry Channon*. Edited by Robert Rhodes James. Harmondsworth: Penguin, 1974, p. 480. Entry for 29 September 1944.

17. Tom Driberg. *Ruling Passions*. London: Jonathan Cape, 1977, p. 186.

18. See, for example, Norman Hart. 'Introducing Terence Rattigan,' *Theatre World*. xxxi, 171. (April 1939). p. 180 or Ruth Jordan. 'Another Adventure Story,' *Woman's Journal*. (August 1949), pp. 31-32.

19. Audrey Williamson. *Theatre of Two Decades*. New York and London: Macmillan, 1951, p. 100.

20. Terence Rattigan. 'Concerning the Play of Ideas,' *New Statesman and Nation*. (4 March 1950), pp. 241-242.

21. Terence Rattigan. 'The Play of Ideas,' *New Statesman and Nation*. (13 May 1950), pp. 545-546. See also Susan Rusinko, 'Rattigan versus Shaw: The 'Drama of Ideas' Debate'. in: *Shaw: The Annual of Bernard Shaw Studies: Volume Two*. Edited by Stanley Weintraub. University Park, Penn: Pennsylvania State University Press, 1982. pp. 171-78.

22. John Elsom writes that Rattigan's plays 'represented establishment writing'. *Post-War British Drama*. Revised Edition. London: Routledge, 1979, p. 33.

23. B. A. Young. *The Rattigan Version: Sir Terence Rattigan and the Theatre of Character*. Hamish Hamilton: London, 1986, pp. 102-103; and Darlow and Hodson, *op. cit.*, p. 196, 204n.

24. Terence Rattigan. *Coll. Plays: Vol. Two. op. cit.*, pp. xi-xii.

25. *Ibid.,* p. xii.

26. *Ibid.,* p. xiv.

27. *Ibid.,* p. xvi.

28. *Ibid.,* p. xviii.

29. Opened on 17 September 1960. cf. *Plays and Players*. vii, 11 (November 1960).

30. Quoted in Irving Wardle. *The Theatres of George Devine*. London: Jonathan Cape, 1978, p. 180.

31. John Osborne. *Almost a Gentleman: An Autobiography, Volume II 1955-1966*. London: Faber and Faber, 1991, p. 20.

32. Robert Muller. 'Soul-Searching with Terence Rattigan.' *Daily Mail*. (30 April 1960).

33. The headline of Hobson's review in the *Sunday Times*, 11 May 1958.

34. See, for example, Nicholas de Jongh. *Not in Front of the Audience: Homosexuality on Stage*. London: Routledge, 1992, pp. 55-58.

35. Kathleen Tynan. *The Life of Kenneth Tynan*. Corrected Edition. London: Methuen, 1988, p. 118.

36. Cf. Jeffrey Weeks. *Coming Out: Homosexual Politics in Britain from the Nineteenth Century to the Present*. Revised and Updated Edition. London and New York: Quartet, 1990, p. 58; Peter Wildeblood. *Against the Law*. London: Weidenfeld and Nicolson, 1955, p. 46. The story of Gielgud's arrest may be found in Huggett, *op. cit.,* pp. 429-431. It was Gielgud's arrest which apparently inspired Rattigan to write the second part of *Separate Tables*, although again, thanks this time to the Lord Chamberlain, Rattigan had to change the Major's offence to a heterosexual one. See Darlow and Hodson, *op. cit.*, p. 228.

37. See, for example, Rodney Garland's novel about homosexual life in London, *The Heart in Exile*. London: W. H. Allen, 1953, p. 104.

38. See note 36; and also 'Rattigan Talks to John Simon,' *Theatre Arts*. 46 (April 1962), p. 24.

39. Terence Rattigan and Anthony Maurice. *Follow my Leader.* Typescript. Lord Chamberlain Play Collection: 1940/2. Box 2506. [British Library].

40. Quoted in Darlow and Hodson, *op. cit.*, p. 15.

41. B. A. Young, *op. cit.*, p. 162.

42. Quoted in Darlow and Hodson, *op. cit.*, p. 56.

43. Quoted in Sheridan Morley, *op. cit.*

44. Darlow and Hodson, *op. cit.*, p. 308.

45. *Guardian*. (2 December 1977).

The Winslow Boy

Terence Rattigan spent much of World War Two working in the
RAF Film Unit, producing a series of semi-propaganda scripts, like
The Day Will Dawn, *Uncensored* and *The Way to the Stars*. It was
his producer from the film unit, Anatole de Grunwald, who suggested
to him shortly before the end of the war that he might get together a
separate proposal for a film looking at British justice. The idea app-
ealed to Rattigan, whose hobbies included collecting books on famous
trials; he and the film director Anthony Asquith used to play a party
game where they staged mock trials around fictional crimes.

Rattigan wanted to write a screenplay arising out of the celebrated
trial in 1910 of George Archer-Shee, a case which 'had so
fascinated and moved me that unlike many ideas that will
peacefully wait in the store-room of the mind until their time for
emergence has come, it demanded instant expression'.¹ But
Grunwald, of the opinion that the episode was rather dull, rejected
it. And when Rattigan peevishly announced that he would write it
as a play instead, Asquith insisted that it would be too expensive,
requiring court and domestic scenes and a huge cast of extras.
Spurred by the scepticism of his two friends, Rattigan set to work.

As befitting his subject, Rattigan decided to write the play in the
sturdy form of the four-act 'well-made play', which had become
the staple of the late Victorian and Edwardian theatre. This has led
one critic to describe *The Winslow Boy* as 'a deliberate, self-
conscious piece of revivalism',² and in a way it is; but the adoption
of this form has theatrical advantages, and Rattigan would no doubt
have argued, like Ronnie Winslow, that copying someone else's
writing is, in itself, also writing. For, while providing a series of
technical devices to introduce the legal story, this model also gives
Rattigan a formal language with which to conjure up a family
living on the other side of two world wars. Avoiding the rather
looser vernacular of his other plays, Rattigan gives several figures a
verbal stiffness which captures the Edwardian Winslows by
echoing the decorous style of Granville Barker or Galsworthy:

> SIR ROBERT. It is interesting to note that the exact words he uses
> on such occasions are: Let Right be done.
>
> ARTHUR. Let Right be done? I like that phrase, sir.
>
> SIR ROBERT. It has a certain ring about it – has it not?
> (*Languidly.*) Let Right be done. (p. 47)

The final act of *The Winslow Boy* recalls the first act of Pinero's *Benefit of the Doubt* (1895), in which a woman waits with her family to hear the result of a petition for separation in which she is cited.[3] An even more persuasive model may be Henry Arthur Jones's *Mrs Dane's Defence* (1900). Mrs Dane is trying to conceal from her small-minded community that she once had an affair with a married man. In Act Three, she is confronted by Sir Daniel Carteret, a barrister with a fearsome reputation for cross-examination, who believes that the secret of someone's guilt may be revealed in 'a look, a gesture, a word, [which] will give you a peep into the very soul of a man or woman'.[4] His blistering interrogation of Mrs Dane may have provided Rattigan with a model for Robert Morton's cross-examination of Ronnie at the end of Act Two.

Rattigan usually wrote by beginning with characters, relationships or ideas, and then developing a plot out of them. For this project, he had, with some difficulty, to invert his usual practice: 'I found it a dreadful task and, after hurling the play many times into my mental wastepaper basket, I decided that the only way that the impossible equation would work out was by dint of some judiciously concealed cheating'.[5] By the Autumn of 1945, as Chips Channon records in his diary, Rattigan was well under way with the piece. Channon recalls suggesting the ghastly title *Ronnie v. Rex*, which Rattigan temporarily adopted.[6] A month later, the play was practically complete, now retitled with Channon's rather better suggestion, *The Winslow Boy*. The play took six and a half weeks to write.[7]

H. M. Tennent Ltd. who had produced Rattigan's previous three plays took on *The Winslow Boy*. The part of Sir Robert Morton was offered to John Gielgud who turned it down, as he would with the part of Andrew Crocker-Harris in *The Browning Version* three years later. Instead the part went to the playwright and actor, Emlyn Williams. After a brief pre-London tour, *The Winslow Boy* opened at the West End's Lyric Theatre, with Frank Cellier and Madge Compton as the mother and father and Angela Baddeley as the suffragette sister. It ran for well over a year and won Rattigan the first of his two Ellen Terry Awards for Best New Play. The following year, the play opened in America, gaining the New York Critics Circle Award for Best Foreign Play.

The Archer-Shee trial concerned a thirteen-year-old cadet at Osborne Naval College, Isle of Wight, accused of stealing a 5/- postal order from another cadet's locker. The boy's high-handed expulsion from Osborne, despite his protestations of innocence, prompted the family to take an action against the Admiralty. Since it was protected by the Crown, the Navy was usually immune from civil actions; however, the Archer-Shees' barrister, Edward Carson, used the exceptional device of a Petition of Right, whereby a citizen could request special permission from the Crown to proceed. In May 1909, Edward VII received the Petition and, using the traditional form of words, signed across it, writing 'Let Right be done', allowing the prosecution to go ahead.[8]

The Admiralty managed to challenge the Petition of Right, but after a successful appeal, the trial opened on 26 July 1910. The boy's frankness and composure in the witness box impressed the court and the proceedings were widely reported. After a series of dramatic cross-examinations and some inauspicious appearances by various Naval officers from Osborne, Sir Rufus Isaacs, the Admiralty's representative, rose on the fourth day of the trial to announce that 'I say now, on behalf of the Admiralty, that I accept the statement of George Archer-Shee that he did not write the name on the postal order, and did not cash it, and consequently that he is innocent of the charge'.[9] As Edward Carson sat with tears in his eyes, members of the jury climbed over the barriers to congratulate members of the family.

The case was quickly drawn into political debate; that afternoon, MPs questioned the First Lord of the Admiralty, Reginald McKenna, arguing that his handling of the case had brought British justice into disrepute. One year later, the Admiralty had still not resolved the issue of damages (for which they may not have been legally responsible); George's brother, a recently elected Conservative and Unionist MP, brought the issue up in the House. Feeling was so strong that the Naval Estimates debate was squeezed to make room for it. After scenes of considerable rancour, McKenna was forced to recommend substantial compensation. In June 1911, the month of Rattigan's birth, the Winslows were awarded £3000 plus costs. No formal letter of withdrawal or apology was ever sent. In a further historical irony, George Archer-Shee was old enough, when war was declared, to be called up. In 1914, an order to withdraw failed to reach his platoon in Ypres, and as they endeavoured to hold the front line, he was killed.

Archer-Shees v. Admiralty was unexceptional in itself, only directly leading to some small amendments in the disciplinary rules in Naval Colleges. But it became a talisman for warring interests, each detecting in the case some echo of their own struggle. The time of the trial was a crossroads at which several debates about the Navy, democracy and representation met. 1910 was one of the most volatile years in British politics this century.

Under the First Sea Lord, the monomaniacal John Fisher, a series of dramatic initiatives had begun to transform Britain's Navy. Not least of these was the commissioning of the Dreadnought in 1905, a huge battleship which rendered most other vessels obsolete. Germany was rapidly rearming and Fisher urged that eight of these ships be built. The Liberal government of the time was more keen on domestic reform; but Fisher, sensing that if Britannia were to rule the waves then Britannia would have to waive the rules, used leaks to manipulate the press and public opinion in favour of his Dreadnought programme.[10] Britain, having seen no major fleet action since the Battle of Trafalgar almost a century before, was rather unused to contemplating its Navy. To find itself propelled suddenly into the political arena, firstly over the Dreadnought and now over Archer-Shee, unsettled this already warring and divided institution even further.

Furthermore, the House of Lords, which at that time could veto any legislation passed by the Commons, were making it impossible for the Liberals to get the programme through. Measures over education, land and licensing laws were having to be withdrawn or face mutilation by the Upper House's 'obscure and far from intelligent peers'.[11] In 1909, Lloyd George, as Chancellor of the Exchequer, put together a 'People's Budget', designed to fund new welfare policies, like the provision of state pensions, that the Liberal government had recently introduced. The funding plans for these measures hit most directly at the wealthy and so it was that when the bill was presented to the Lords, they rejected it. Two years of elections, debates and constitutional crisis were finally brought to an end when, in August 1911, mindful of Asquith's promise that five hundred new peers would be created to flood the Upper House, the Lords voted away their historic veto.

The campaign for women's suffrage was on the threshold of its most fierce period of agitation. Riding on a century of increasing demand for the vote, the National Union of Women's Suffrage Societies (1897), led by Millicent Fawcett, and the Women's Social and Political Union (1903), led by Emmeline Pankhurst, were formed. From 1906, the WPSU had led a more and more militant campaign, breaking up meetings, smashing windows, carrying out acts of arson, and – rather wittily – burning 'Votes for Women' into the grass of golf courses around the country. However, in July 1910, as George Archer-Shee stood in the witness box, the WPSU were holding back. A new bill, framed by an all-party committee, which would have enfranchised one million women, had passed its first and second reading. But their hopes faded when Asquith announced a procedural move, designed to prevent any further progress of the legislation through the Commons. The bill was lost.

The Suffragettes transformed this moment of huge disillusionment into a source of political energy and from here on their campaign became increasingly violent and bitter. What also marks the next four years is the savagery of the response to these women. The end of 1910 saw 'Black Friday' where a peaceful deputation of women to Parliament was physically abused and beaten by the police. And when imprisoned suffragettes, demanding to be treated as political prisoners, began hunger strikes, they were brutally force fed, through the mouth, nose and sometimes anus. And as the cruelty of this treatment began to reach public ears, Reginald McKenna, now Home Secretary, introduced the 'Cat and Mouse' Acts whereby suffragette prisoners would continually be released and re-arrested.[12]

The ambivalence of the Liberal government, which could fight tooth and nail to force legislation it was elected to introduce through parliament but also slither and twist in its desire to evade the demands for women's suffrage, provides a considerably more unstable context for the Archer-Shee case than is often suggested. Far from being a simple moral lesson in 'the inviolable sovereignty of the individual',[13] the trial was threaded through with ambivalences and tensions, which also provide Rattigan with traces that deepen and trouble *The Winslow Boy*.

That a play set in this turbulent period of British political history should have been written in 1945 is not surprising. The Labour government, elected in July that year, was pledged to introduce the most radical and comprehensive series of social reforms that the country had seen for over a century. And yet the roots of much of this legislation, with its decisive abandonment of the nineteenth-century *laissez-faire* tradition, lay in the Liberal administrations of 1906-1914, in their development of state provisions for pensions, unemployment and health insurance. Indeed the man most closely responsible for framing the national insurance legislation, William Beveridge, had been responsible for designing and popularising the national system of 'Labour Exchanges' which began operating in 1909.[14]

The landslide Labour victory had shocked many in Rattigan's circle, notably Henry 'Chips' Channon. But Rattigan did not share entirely in his Conservative friends' dismay. Under the influence of Anthony Asquith, son of the former Prime Minister, he had moved towards the Liberals.[15] And his use of the source material is notable for its underplaying of the Tories rôle in fighting for George's innocence. In one notable piece of 'judiciously concealed cheating', he transformed the conservative Winslow daughter, Catherine, into a suffragette, and George's thirty-six year old elder brother, the Tory MP Major Martin Archer-Shee, into the under-graduate 'silly ass' Dickie Winslow. Indeed, when the play's pre-London tour came to Bristol, Rattigan had to take the still-living daughter to lunch and persuade her to accept his redrafting of her life.[16] The names of most of the characters have been altered (George becomes Ronnie Winslow, his parents Grace and Arthur, and Edward Carson is now Robert Morton) giving Rattigan room to widen the scope and implications of the case.

The play's contemporary relevance was noted by the critics, and Rattigan uses the benefits of hindsight to place delicate layers of irony upon the Archer-Shee story. While his adoption of the 'well-made play' structure has its own historical resonances, by displacing the action of the play from the court room to the home, Rattigan is able to present a set of wider emotional concerns that reflect upon and complicate the otherwise sentimental story of the boy pitted against the Admiralty. One thing that is notable about the play is how little Ronnie appears in it at all. He spends most of Act One standing in the garden, most of Act Three asleep and misses the trial in Act Four altogether. His climactic cross-examination at the hands of Robert Morton in Act Two represents his moment of most intense focus, and yet this sequence lasts barely five minutes of stage time. His ambivalent position within the play is captured in the title, which connotes both Ronnie's centrality to the story, and his personal marginality within it.

In fact, *The Winslow Boy* seems more interested in the family and Robert Morton. As Arthur Winslow loses his health, Dickie his undergraduate career and Catherine her fiancé, Grace asks Arthur what he is really doing it for:

> ARTHUR. (*Quietly.*) For Justice, Grace.

> GRACE. That sounds very noble. Are you sure it's true? Are you sure it isn't just plain pride and self-importance and sheer brute stubbornness?

> ARTHUR. (*Putting a hand out.*) No, Grace. I don't think it is. I really don't think it is –

> GRACE. (*Shaking off his hand.*) No. This time I'm not going to cry and say I'm sorry, and make it all up again. I can stand anything if there's a reason for it. But for no reason at all, it's unfair to ask so much of me. (p. 60)

Grace's desperate attempts to preserve familial 'normality' indicate the complex interplay of private and public that weaves through so much of Rattigan's work. And Grace's doubts are supported by the presentation of Arthur. On his first appearance, Rattigan describes him as having a 'deliberately cultured patriarchal air' (p. 5) as he takes up the position of head of the family, with his back to the fireplace. When John Watherstone appears to ask his permission to marry Catherine, elaborate – and somewhat farcical – arrangements are made to clear space for Arthur to discuss financial arrangements with the young suitor. Much of the first act revolves around the fearful responses of other members of the family, not wanting to be around when Arthur hears of Ronnie's dismissal. Rattigan observes well the tensions and absurdities of this traditional family: John's smirk at Desmond, having 'won' Catherine's hand (p. 20), Arthur's dismissive remarks about Grace's 'superstitious terrors' (p. 24) and his, at times, absurd formality (when he discovers that Ronnie has been expelled he orders Dickie to order Violet to order Ronnie to come downstairs). In depicting the family, Rattigan is careful to trace the play of male proprietorial gazes through which the women have to pass.

And Rattigan's keen delineation of this family sets up parallels which open up the simplistic court room drama that is unfolding. Intriguingly, while we never see a moment of the trial, the spirit of cross-examination pervades the play; Sir Robert's interrogation of Ronnie is anticipated in Arthur's financial questioning of John and his threatening appraisal of Ronnie at the end of the first act: 'if you tell me a lie, I shall know it, because a lie between you and me can't be hidden' (p. 28). Ronnie, moving from Admiralty to his father to Sir Robert, is passed from interrogation to interrogation; what links all of these is their patriarchal ferocity, their implacable and arbitrary decisions of right and wrong. Sir Robert's sudden decision that Ronnie is innocent and Arthur's firm belief that the inaudible Vicar is nonetheless a good man are part of a pattern of imperious decision-making that echoes the original, peremptory decision of the Admiralty. Through continual references to the emotional, physical and financial cost of the court case, Rattigan never lets Arthur's particular interests shape the entirety of our experience of this family.

The play offers an alternative perspective in the character of Catherine. Her coolly political perspective gives her a certain distance from the family (when the Winslows first appear she exempts herself from the conversation to read a Trade Union leader's memoirs); and it is Catherine who voices the debate that dominates so much of the play's interest in the story: the distinction between the technical employment of the law and her passionate advocacy of human rights. As so often with Rattigan, the play attempts to negotiate the relations between heart and head, this time focused between and within the characters of Catherine and Morton.

The debate hangs on their two confrontations in Acts Two and Four. Rattigan, while allowing us considerable sympathy for Sir Robert, subtly weights the argument on Catherine's side. While Robert and Arthur are exclusively focused on the narrow issue of 'fact', Catherine sees this is a secondary (and finally unprovable) concern beside the broader issue of how power is deployed: 'His innocence or guilt aren't important to me. They are to my father. Not to me. I believe he didn't do it; but I may be wrong . . . All I care about is that people should know that a Government Department has ignored a fundamental human right and that it should be forced to acknowledge it' (p.71). When the barrister appears at the Winslow home, she challenges him, referring ironically to one of his 'great forensic triumphs', his 'masterly' cross-examination of Len Rogers, a Trade Union leader. 'I suppose you know,' she remarks, 'that he committed suicide a few months ago?' (p. 46). Rogers may be based on Joseph Wilson, founder of the National Union of Seamen, whose attempt to sue the *Evening News* for libel in 1893 was thwarted by his brutal cross-examination at the hands of Carson. But another incident that haunts this moment is Carson's most famous court room appearance: his interrogation of Oscar Wilde, during his libel case against the Marquis of Queensberry. After Carson's remorseless pursuit of Wilde, the case was lost, paving the way for Queensberry's counter-action, and Wilde's imprisonment and disgrace.

The two characters do seem to swap places during the play. Sir Robert, whom Catherine described as 'a fish, a hard, cold-blooded, supercilious, sneering fish' (p. 63), is revealed to have forgone the post of Lord Chief Justice to pursue the case, and to have cried when the verdict was announced. Earlier in the play Dickie had cautioned Catherine not to be too vocal about her political opinions ('Men don't like 'em in their lady friends, even if they agree with 'em') but Catherine is unconcerned: 'If there's ever a clash between what I believe and what I feel, there's not much doubt about which will win' (p. 32). While implying that Catherine may choose heart over head, Rattigan characteristically leaves the statement open. And finally, when her fiancé's father tries to force the family to drop the proceedings, Catherine discovers that her political engagement wins out over her affection for John. Sir Robert's unwilling revelation of emotional engagement in the case is counterpointed by Catherine's decision not to give in to her considerable emotional pressures. Although Catherine admits to not being a militant, this may be seen in the historical context of the Archer-Shee case when, as recounted above, the British suffrage movement was holding back from direct action as Asquith's government seemed on the point of introducing a limited vote for women. It was after this was reneged upon that the Suffragette Movement entered its most radical and militant phase. Catherine's kind of feminism is contrasted with the frivolity of Miss Barnes's trivializing article (a kind of journalism to which Rattigan was himself often subjected).[17]

The final discussion between Robert and Catherine has sometimes been seen as a moment of compromise where left and right meet in some vague middle ground to admire the integrity of each other's political stance. But perhaps this is only half of the picture. While certainly Catherine becomes aware that Sir Robert has made some emotional investment in the case, his airy talk of Right as a form of absolute moral value is still undermined by his condescending opposition to women having the vote, and his unshakeable certainty that it is a 'lost cause' (p. 95). In 1946, almost twenty years after women were fully granted the vote on equal terms with men, Catherine's progressive position would have been apparent, leaving Robert Morton's *soi-disant* objectivity tainted by his own less than liberal convictions. For the audience in 1946, then, this is a play that cautioned against complacency and criticized claims of moral neutrality in favour of a continual compassionate questioning of assumptions. The play has a considerably more complex relation to the new Labour government of 1945 than some critics have suggested.

For the first time, the critics began to recognize Rattigan's complexity and skill, and that his apparently uncomplicated, well-made plays artfully concealed levels of narrative sophistication. Here, the tautly constructed first act interweaves different layers of plot driving the narrative on. Ronnie's appearance opens the play but when the family arrive back from church the plot focuses on Catherine's engagement and the network of responses to it. All the while, however, we are reminded of Ronnie's distressed presence by continual references to the rain and Grace's glimpse of a boy in the garden. The choreographing of the characters, and the slow spread of information, is expertly handled, culminating in the tense moment where Arthur is read Ronnie's letter.

The first critics saw *The Winslow Boy* as a political play, the *Daily Mail* describing it as 'Mr Rattigan's tract for these particular times' and the *Observer* arguing that he 'has vigorously wedded doctrine and drama'.[18] Rattigan's sophisticated ambiguities in the play lead several critics to duck out of a full statement of what this doctrine is, most proffering vague statements about the 'liberty of the individual' (*Observer*). Emlyn Williams was initially given only tentative praise, some feeling that he was not quite able to convey Sir Robert's authority, although his performance was looked back on more warmly. All praised the Act Two curtain when the barrister unexpectedly accepts the brief, and generally critics found the play 'intensely exciting' (*Sunday Times*). Some found that the play was straying somewhat from what they perceived to be its main theme, and *The Times* found that after the verdict is announced, 'the play flickers uncertainly to its end'.

Like many of Rattigan's plays it was many years before London saw a professional revival, though it has always been a staple in regional repertory, with performances in Sheffield (1948), Nottingham (1961), Dundee (1969) and the Bristol Old Vic (1977), among many others; and in 1948, Robert Donat was admired as Robert Morton in a film adaptation, directed and co-scripted by the two men whose scepticism had helped inspire the project, Asquith and Grunwald. The film itself, also starring Margaret Leighton, Cedric Hardwicke and Marie Lohr, was a commercial success, even if, by taking the audience into the courtroom, it muddies the stage play's delicate shifts in focus.

By 1970, London theatre had changed dramatically; the new, experimental, *avant-garde* fringe was achieving mainstream

recognition in the Royal Court's 'Come Together' Festival, as a
revival of *The Winslow Boy*, directed by Frith Banbury, starring
Kenneth More as Sir Robert, Laurence Naismith as Arthur and
Annette Crosbie as Catherine, opened at the New Theatre. Most of
the reviews focused upon seeing how Rattigan sized up in this new,
hostile environment. Ronald Bryden mourned 'the playwright we
lost to permissiveness' (*Observer*) and Philip Hope-Wallace found
that 'the effectiveness of the dramatic method has not been found
to have slipped or rusted' (*Guardian*).[19] This faith was not
universally shared by any means, Irving Wardle finding no pleasure
in the craftsmanship – or 'cunning tricks' as he somewhat back-
handedly describes it – other than 'watching the wheels go round'
(*Times*).[20] It was Albert Hunt, standard bearer of the new
generation, who denounced Rattigan's craft as 'over-rated', 'a
succession of rather clumsy devices' which consist in 'setting up
the obvious in a rather laborious way'. But underlying Wardle and
Hunt's criticisms was the belief that Rattigan's politics were lazy
and complacent, based, as Hunt argued, on 'facile knowingness',
presenting 'a world in which everything can be solved by a little
craftsmanship'.[21]

In 1983, when Michael Rudman revived the play at the Lyric
Theatre, Hammersmith, Benedict Nightingale also saw the play as
a little 'complacent', but was surprised to detect what the first
critics did not, that the final scene 'emerges . . . as the moral climax
of the evening' (*New Statesman*).[22] And his political misgivings
were now not widely shared. For *Time Out*, it 'remains as
contentious and relevant as ever'. All of the critics praised the
'intelligent, detailed production' (*Standard*), describing Rudman's
'beautifully paced' direction (*Guardian*). What emerged more
clearly from this production was the importance of Catherine,
revealed in a strong performance by Diane Fletcher, and the way
that Rattigan hints at Arthur's self-indulgence as he 'begins to bask
in the limelight that has unexpectedly broken in on the chilly dusk
of his retirement' (*Sunday Telegraph*). In 1994 the play was revived
again in the West End, directed by Wyn Jones. The production
caught well the comic elements of the play (notably in Ian
Thompson's forlorn Desmond Curry), and Peter Barkworth's
Arthur was a more amiable, less frightening figure than in previous
productions. Simon Williams as Robert Morton brought a breath of
icy, aloof cynicism into his debates with Eve Matheson's playful
but alert Catherine. As the play went on, the decline of the family
was reflected in the shadows which blanketed more and more of the
Winslows' drawing room.

In America, Rattigan resisted urgings to give the play a rounder
ending by suggesting romance between Sir Robert and Catherine,[23]
and still achieved his first real Broadway success. Howard Barnes
found it 'a work of scope, imagination and cumulative emotional
power' (*New York Herald Tribune*), Robert Coleman praised 'a

play notable for integrity, honesty and decent emotion' (*New York Daily Mirror*), and William Hawkins called it 'compelling, suspenseful and inspiring' (*New York World Telegram*). Most agreed that it was 'beyond dispute the best play he has so far written'.[24] The cast was uniformly praised, one critic noting that 'the repressed pathos of the British stiff upper-lip [which] can sometimes be uncomfortable in the theatre' is overcome by performances that give it 'a completely credible air of gallantry' (*New York Post*). Some critics were less delighted, two of them linking its perceived dramatic poverty with the financial crisis in Britain, part induced by America's sudden withdrawal of wartime credit (*New York Daily News*, *New York Journal-American*). The cruellest review was Louis Kronenberger's in *PM*, which dismissed the play as 'meretricious . . . evidence of an incorrigibly trashy mind'.[25] The play also received an unusually successful Off-Broadway revival in the early eighties, which led one critic to enthuse that 'it has a plot . . . that moves forward ineluctably yet suspensefully, with exemplary crafted changes of pace; characters that, however peripheral, bulge with foreshortened but three-dimensional palpability; and, loveliest of all, areas of unstated possibility – opened but unfilled – in vistas where the audience's imagination is allowed free, creative play'.[26]

Rattigan once remarked that if *The Browning Version* was his passport to heaven, *The Winslow Boy* was the leather wallet which contained it.[27] It marked the beginning of a ten-year period in which Rattigan's premières received serious critical attention. Recognition began to grow of the scope of his ambitions, the sensitivity of his craft and the complexity of his emotional choreography.   DAN REBELLATO

Notes

I would like to thank the staff of the Theatre Museum, London, for their help in tracing revivals and reviews of *The Winslow Boy*.

1. Terence Rattigan. Preface. *The Collected Plays of Terence Rattigan: Volume One*. London: Hamish Hamilton, 1953, p. xvii.

2. John Russell Taylor. *The Rise and Fall of the Well-Made Play*. London: Methuen, 1967. p. 151.

3. Arthur Wing Pinero. *The Benefit of the Doubt*. (Plays: XIV). London: Heinemann, 1896.

4. Henry Arthur Jones. *Mrs Dane's Defence*. in: *Representative Plays: Volume Three*. Edited by Clayton Hamilton. London: Macmillan, 1926. p. 214.

5. Terence Rattigan. 'How I Write My Plays.' *Strand Magazine*. cxii, 674. (February 1947), p. 97.

6. Henry Channon. *Chips: The Diaries of Sir Henry Channon*. Ed. Robert Rhodes James. Harmondsworth: Penguin, 1974, p. 502. Entry for 19 Aug. 1945.

7. *ibid.*, p. 504. Entry for 17 September 1945.

8. See Rodney M. Bennett. *The Archer-Shees Against the Admiralty: The Story Behind 'The Winslow Boy'*. London: Robert Hale, 1973.

9. *Ibid.*, p. 129.

10. Colin Cross. *The Liberals in Power 1905-1914*. London: Barrie and Rockliff-Pall Mall Press, 1963, pp. 98-99.

11. George Dangerfield. *The Strange Death of Liberal England*. London: Constable, 1936, p. 20.

12. See Jill Liddington and Jill Norris. *One Hand Tied Behind Us: The Rise of the Women's Suffrage Movement*. London: Virago, 1978, and Midge Mackenzie. *Shoulder to Shoulder: A Documentary*. New York: Knopf, 1975.

13. Alexander Woollcott. *Long, Long Ago*. London: Cassell, 1945. p. 116.

14. See Peter Hennessy. *Never Again: Britain 1945-1951*. London: Vintage, 1993. pp. 126-127, and Cross, *op. cit.,* p. 87.

15. Michael Darlow and Gillian Hodson. *Terence Rattigan: The Man and His Work*. London and New York: Quartet Books, 1979. p. 267.

16. *Ibid.*, p. 147.

17. See, for example, Ruth Jordan. 'Another Adventure Story,' *Woman's Journal*. (August 1949), pp. 31-32, which spends as much time describing his Albany furnishings as it does discussing his plays.

18. Production File for *The Winslow Boy*, Lyric Theatre. 23 May 1946, in the Theatre Museum, London.

19. Bryden, quoted in Darlow and Hodson, *op. cit.*, p. 284. Philip Hope Wallace. 'Review: *The Winslow Boy*,' *The Guardian*. (6 November 1970), p. 8.

20. Irving Wardle. 'Review: *The Winslow Boy*,' *The Times*. (6 November 1970), p. 13.

21. Albert Hunt. 'Danger: Craftsman at Work.' *New Society*. xvi, 424. (12 November 1970). p. 873.

22. Reviews drawn from *London Theatre Record*, iii, 13 (18 June-1 July 1983), p. 513ff and also iii, 14/15 (2-29 July 1983), p. 578.

23. Darlow and Hodson, *op. cit.*, p. 148.

24. John Mason Brown. *Seeing More Things*. London: Hamilton, 1949. p. 38.

25. Broadway reviews quoted, unless otherwise indicated, from *New York Critics' Reviews*. viii, 17 (3 November 1947), pp. 283-286.

26. John Simon in *New York Magazine*, quoted in Holly Hill. 'Rattigan's Renaissance.' *Contemporary Review*. ccxxxx, 1392. (January 1982). p. 38.

27. Richard Huggett. *Binkie Beaumont: Eminence Grise of the West Theatre 1933-1973*. London: Hodder & Stoughton, 1989. p. 363.

List of Rattigan's Produced Plays

Title	British Première	New York Première
First Episode (with Philip Heimann)	'Q' Theatre, Surrey, 11 Sept 1933, trans. Comedy Th, 26 January 1934	Ritz Theatre 17 September 1934
French Without Tears	Criterion Th, 6 Nov 1936	Henry Miller Th, 28 Sept 1937
After the Dance	St James's Th, 21 June 1939	
Follow My Leader (with Anthony Maurice, alias Tony Goldschmidt)	Apollo Th, 16 Jan 1940	
Grey Farm (with Hector Bolitho)		Hudson Th, 3 May 1940
Flare Path	Apollo Th, 13 Aug 1942	Henry Miller Th, 23 Dec 1942
While the Sun Shines	Globe Th, 24 Dec 1943	Lyceum Th, 19 Sept 1944
Love in Idleness	Lyric Th, 20 Dec 1944	Empire Th (as *O Mistress Mine*), 23 Jan 1946
The Winslow Boy	Lyric Th, 23 May 1946	Empire Th, 29 October 1947
Playbill (The Browning Version, Harlequinade)	Phoenix Th, 8 Sept 1948	Coronet Th, 12 October 1949
Adventure Story	St James's Th, 17 March 1949	
A Tale of Two Cities (adapt from Dickens, with John Gielgud)	St Brendan's College Dramatic Scy, Clifton, 23 Jan 1950	
Who is Sylvia?	Criterion Th, 24 Oct 1950	
Final Test (tv)	BBC TV 29 July 1951	

The Deep Blue Sea	Duchess Th, 6 March 1952	Morosco Th, 5 Nov 1952
The Sleeping Prince	Phoenix Th, 5 November 1953	Coronet Th, 1 November 1956
Separate Tables (*Table by the Window, Table Number Seven*)	St James's Th, 22 Sept 1954	Music Box Th, 25 Oct 1956
Variation on a Theme	Globe Th, 8 May 1958	
Ross	Theatre Royal, Haymarket, 12 May 1960	Eugene O'Neill Th, 26 Dec 1961
Joie de Vivre (with Robert Stolz, Paul Dehn)	Queen's Th, 14 July 1960	
Heart to Heart (tv)	BBC TV, 6 Dec 1962	
Man and Boy	Queen's Th, 4 Sept 1963	Brooks Atkinson Th, 12 Nov 1963
Ninety Years On (tv)	BBC TV, 29 Nov 1964	
Nelson – a Portrait in Miniature (tv)	Associated Television, 21 March 1966	
All on Her Own (tv) [adapted for stage as *Duologue*]	BBC 2, 25 Sept 1968 King's Head, Feb 1976	
A Bequest to the Nation	Theatre Royal, Haymarket, 23 Sept 1970	
High Summer (tv)	Thames TV, 12 Sept 1972	
In Praise of Love (*After Lydia, Before Dawn*)	Duchess Th, 27 Sept 1973	Morosco Th, 10 Dec 1974
Cause Célèbre (radio)	BBC Radio 4 27 Oct 1975	
Cause Célèbre (stage)	Her Majesty's Th, 4 July 1977	

THE WINSLOW BOY

Act One	A Sunday morning in July
Act Two	An evening in April (nine months later)
Act Three	An evening in January (nine months later)
Act Four	An afternoon in June (five months later)

The action of the play takes place in Arthur Winslow's house in Kensington, London, and extends over two years preceding the war of 1914-1918.

The Winslow Boy was first produced at the Lyric Theatre, London, on 23 May 1946, with the following cast:

RONNIE WINSLOW	Michael Newell
VIOLET	Kathleen Harrison
ARTHUR WINSLOW	Frank Cellier
GRACE WINSLOW	Madge Compton
DICKIE WINSLOW	Jack Watling
CATHERINE WINSLOW	Angela Baddeley
JOHN WATHERSTONE	Alastair Bannerman
DESMOND CURRY	Clive Morton
MISS BARNES	Mona Washbourne
FRED	Brian Harding
SIR ROBERT MORTON	Emlyn Williams

The play directed by Glen Byam Shaw

Act One

Scene: The drawing-room of a house in Courtfield Gardens, South Kensington, on a morning in July, at some period not long before the war of 1914-1918.

The furnishings betoken solid but not undecorative upper middle-class comfort.

On the rise of the curtain A BOY of about fourteen, dressed in the uniform of an Osborne naval cadet, is discovered. There is something rigid and tense in his attitude, and his face is blank and without expression.

There is the sound of someone in the hall. As the sound comes nearer, he looks despairingly round, as if contemplating flight. An elderly maid (VIOLET) comes in, and stops in astonishment at sight of him.

VIOLET. Master Ronnie!

RONNIE. (*With ill-managed sang-froid.*) Hello, Violet.

VIOLET. Why, good gracious! We weren't expecting you back till Tuesday.

RONNIE. Yes, I know.

VIOLET. Why ever didn't you let us know you were coming, you silly boy? Your mother should have been at the station to meet you. The idea of a child like you wandering all over London by yourself. I never did. However did you get in? By the garden, I suppose.

RONNIE. No. The front-door. I rang and cook opened it.

VIOLET. And where's your trunk and your tuck box?

RONNIE. Upstairs. The taximan carried them up –

VIOLET. Taximan? You took a taxi?

RONNIE *nods.*

All by yourself? Well, I don't know what little boys are coming to, I'm sure. What your father and mother will say, I don't know

RONNIE. Where are they, Violet?

VIOLET. Church, of course.

RONNIE. (*Vacantly.*) Oh, yes. It's Sunday, isn't it?

VIOLET. What's the matter with you? What have they been doing to you at Osborne?

RONNIE. (*Sharply.*) What do you mean?

VIOLET. They seem to have made you a bit soft in the head, or something. Well – I suppose I'd better get your unpacking done – Mr. Dickie's been using your chest of drawers for all his dress clothes and things. I'll just clear 'em out and put 'em on his bed – that's what I'll do. He can find room for 'em somewhere else.

RONNIE. Shall I help you?

VIOLET. (*Scornfully.*) I know *your* help. With *your* help I'll be at it all day. No, you just wait down here for your mother and father. They'll be back in a minute.

RONNIE *nods and turns hopelessly away.* VIOLET *looks at his retreating back, puzzled.*

Well?

RONNIE. (*Turning.*) Yes?

VIOLET. Don't I get a kiss or are you too grown up for that now?

RONNIE. Sorry, Violet.

He goes up to her and is enveloped in her ample bosom.

VIOLET. That's better. My, what a big boy you're getting!

She holds him at arm's length and inspects him.

Quite the little naval officer, aren't you?

RONNIE. (*Smiling forlornly.*) Yes. That's right.

VIOLET. Well, well – I must be getting on –

She goes out. RONNIE, left alone, resumes his attitude of utter dejection. He takes out of his pocket a letter in a sealed envelope. After a second's hesitation, he opens it, and reads the contents. The perusal appears to increase his misery.

He makes for a moment as if to tear it up; then changes his mind again, and puts it back in his pocket. He gets up and takes two or three quick steps towards the hall door. Then he stops, uncertainly.

There is the sound of voices in the hall. RONNIE jumps to his feet; then, with a strangled sob runs to the garden door, and down the iron steps into the garden.

The hall door opens and the rest of the Winslow family file in. They are ARTHUR and GRACE – Ronnie's father and mother – and DICKIE *and* CATHERINE *– his brother and sister. All are carrying prayerbooks, and wear that faintly unctuous after-church air.*

ARTHUR *leans heavily on a stick. He is a man of about sixty, with a rather deliberately cultured patriarchal air.* GRACE *is about ten years younger, with the faded remnants of prettiness.* DICKIE *is an Oxford undergraduate, large, noisy, and cheerful.* CATHERINE, *approaching thirty, has an air of masculinity about her which is at odd variance with her mother's intense femininity.*

GRACE. (*As she enters.*) – But he's so old, dear. From the back of the church you really can't hear a word he says –

ARTHUR. He's a good man, Grace.

GRACE. But what's the use of being good, if you're inaudible?

CATHERINE. A problem in ethics for you, Father.

ARTHUR *is standing with his back to fireplace. He looks round at the open garden door.*

ARTHUR. There's a draught, Grace.

GRACE *goes to the door and closes it.*

GRACE. Oh, dear – it's coming on to rain.

DICKIE. I'm on Mother's side. The old boy's so doddery now he can hardly finish the course at all. I timed him today. It took him seventy-five seconds dead from a flying start to reach the pulpit, and then he needed the whip coming round the bend. I call that pretty bad going.

ARTHUR. I don't think that's very funny, Richard.

DICKIE. Oh, don't you, Father?

ARTHUR. Doddery though Mr. Jackson may seem now, I very much doubt if he failed in his pass mods. when he was at Oxford.

DICKIE. (*Aggrieved.*) Dash it – Father – you promised not to mention that again this vac –

GRACE. You did, you know, Arthur.

ARTHUR. There was a condition to my promise – if you remember – that Dickie should provide me with reasonable evidence of his intentions to work.

DICKIE. Well, haven't I, Father? Didn't I stay in all last night – a Saturday night – and work?

ARTHUR. You stayed in, Dickie. I would be the last to deny that.

GRACE. You *were* making rather a noise, dear, with that old gramophone of yours. I really can't believe you could have been doing much work with that going on all the time –

DICKIE. Funnily enough, Mother, it helps me to concentrate –

ARTHUR. Concentrate on what?

DICKIE. Work, of course.

ARTHUR. That was not what you appeared to be concentrating on when I came down to fetch a book – sleep, may I say, having been rendered out of the question by the hideous sounds emanating from this room.

DICKIE. Edwina and her father had just looked in on their way to the Graham's dance – they only stayed a minute –

GRACE. What an idiotic girl that is! Oh, sorry, Dickie – I was forgetting. You're rather keen on her, aren't you?

ARTHUR. You would have had ample proof of that fact, Grace, if you had seen them in the attitude I caught them in last night.

DICKIE. We were practising the Bunny Hug.

GRACE. The what, dear?

DICKIE. The Bunny Hug. It's the new dance.

CATHERINE. (*Helpfully.*) It's like the Turkey Trot – only more dignified.

GRACE. I thought that was the tango.

DICKIE. No. More like a Fox Trot, really. Something between a Boston Glide and a Kangaroo Hop.

ARTHUR. We appear to be straying from the point. Whatever animal was responsible for the posture I found you in does not alter the fact that you have not done one single stroke of work this vacation.

DICKIE. Oh. Well, I do work awfully fast, you know – once I get down to it.

ARTHUR. That assumption can hardly be based on experience, I take it.

DICKIE. Dash it, Father! You are laying in to me this morning.

ARTHUR. It's time you found out, Dickie, that I'm not spending two hundred pounds a year keeping you at Oxford, merely to learn to dance the Bunny Hop.

DICKIE. Hug, Father.

ARTHUR. The exact description of the obscenity is immaterial.

GRACE. Father's quite right, you know, dear. You really have been going the pace a bit, this vac.

DICKIE. Yes, I know, Mother – but the season's nearly over now –

GRACE. (*With a sigh.*) I wish you were as good about work as Ronnie.

DICKIE. (*Hotly.*) I like that. That's a bit thick, I must say. All Ronnie ever has to do with his footling little homework is to add two and two.

ARTHUR. Ronnie is at least proving a good deal more successful in adding two and two than you were at his age.

DICKIE. (*Now furious.*) Oh, yes. *I* know. *I* know. *He* got into Osborne and *I* failed. That's going to be brought up again –

GRACE. Nobody's bringing it up, dear –

DICKIE. Oh, yes they are. It's going to be brought up against me all my life. Ronnie's the good little boy, I'm the bad little boy. You've just stuck a couple of labels on us that nothing on earth is ever going to change.

GRACE. Don't be so absurd, dear –

DICKIE. It's not absurd. It's quite true. Isn't it, Kate?

CATHERINE *looks up from a book she has been reading in the corner.*

CATHERINE. I'm sorry, Dickie. I haven't been listening. Isn't what quite true?

DICKIE. That in the eyes of Mother and Father nothing that Ronnie does is ever wrong, and nothing I do is ever right?

CATHERINE. (*After a pause.*) If I were you, Dickie dear, I d go and have a nice lie down before lunch.

DICKIE. (*After a further pause.*) Perhaps you're right.

He goes towards the hall door.

ARTHUR. If you're going to your room I suggest you take that object with you.

He points to a gramophone – 1912 model, with horn – lying on a table.

It's out of place in a drawing-room.

DICKIE, *with an air of hauteur, picks up the gramophone and carries it to the door.*

It might help you to concentrate on the work you're going to do this afternoon.

DICKIE *stops at the door, and then turns slowly.*

DICKIE. (*With dignity.*) That is out of the question, I'm afraid.

ARTHUR. Indeed? Why?

DICKIE. I have an engagement with Miss Gunn.

ARTHUR. On a Sunday afternoon? Escorting her to the National Gallery, no doubt?

DICKIE. No. The Victoria and Albert Museum.

He goes out with as much dignity as is consistent with the carrying of a very bulky gramophone.

GRACE. How stupid of him to say that about labels. There's no truth in it at all – is there, Kate?

CATHERINE. (*Deep in her book.*) No, Mother.

GRACE. Oh, dear, it's simply pelting. What are you reading, Kate?

CATHERINE. Len Rogers's Memoirs.

GRACE. Who's Len Rogers?

CATHERINE. A Trades Union Leader.

GRACE. Does John know you're a Radical?

CATHERINE. Oh, yes.

GRACE. And a Suffragette?

CATHERINE. Certainly.

GRACE. (*With a smile.*) And he still wants to marry you?

CATHERINE. He seems to.

GRACE. Oh, by the way, I've asked him to come early for lunch – so that he can have a few words with Father first.

CATHERINE. Good idea. I hope you've been primed, have you Father?

ARTHUR. (*Who has been nearly asleep.*) What's that?

CATHERINE. You know what you're going to say to John, don't you? You're not going to let me down and forbid the match, or anything, are you? Because I warn you, if you do, I shall elope –

ARTHUR. (*Taking her hand.*) Never fear, my dear. I'm far too delighted at the prospect of getting you off our hands at last.

CATHERINE. (*Smiling.*) I'm not sure I like that 'at last'.

GRACE. Do you love him, dear?

CATHERINE. John? Yes, I do.

GRACE. You're such a funny girl. You never show your feelings much, do you? You don't behave as if you were in love.

CATHERINE. How does one behave as if one is in love?

ARTHUR. One doesn't read Len Rogers. One reads Byron.

CATHERINE. I do both.

ARTHUR. An odd combination.

CATHERINE. A satisfying one.

GRACE. I meant – you don't talk about him much, do you?

CATHERINE. No. I suppose I don't.

GRACE. (*Sighing.*) I don't think you modern girls have the feelings our generation did. It's this New Woman attitude.

CATHERINE. Very well, Mother. I love John in every way that a woman can love a man, and far, far more than he loves me. Does that satisfy you?

GRACE. (*Embarrassed.*) Well, really, Kate darling – I didn't ask for anything quite like that – (*To* ARTHUR.) What are you laughing at, Arthur?

ARTHUR. (*Chuckling.*) One up to the New Woman.

GRACE. Nonsense. She misunderstood me, that's all. (*At the window.*) Just look at the rain! (*Turning to* CATHERINE.) Kate, darling, does Desmond know about you and John?

CATHERINE. I haven't told him. On the other hand, if he hasn't guessed, he must be very dense.

ARTHUR. He is very dense.

GRACE. Oh, no. He's quite clever, if you really get under his skin.

ARTHUR. Oddly enough, I've never had that inclination.

GRACE. I think he's a dear. Kate darling, you *will* be kind to him, won't you?

CATHERINE. (*Patiently.*) Yes, Mother. Of course I will.

GRACE. He's really a very good sort –

She breaks off suddenly and stares out of the window.

Hullo! There's someone in our garden.

CATHERINE. (*Coming to look.*) Where?

GRACE. (*Pointing.*) Over there, do you see?

CATHERINE. No.

GRACE. He's just gone behind that bush. It was a boy, I think. Probably Mrs. Williamson's awful little Dennis.

CATHERINE. (*Leaving the window.*) Well, whoever it is must be getting terribly wet.

GRACE. Why can't he stick to his own garden?

There is a sound of voices outside in the hall.

GRACE. Was that John?

CATHERINE. It sounded like it.

GRACE. (*After listening.*) Yes. It's John. (*To* CATHERINE.) Quick! In the dining-room!

CATHERINE. All right.

She dashes across to the dining-room door.

GRACE. Here! You've forgotten your bag.

She darts to the table and picks it up.

ARTHUR. (*Startled.*) What on earth is going on?

GRACE. (*In a stage whisper.*) We're leaving you alone with John. When you've finished cough or something.

ARTHUR. (*Testily.*) What do you mean, or something?

GRACE. I know. Knock on the floor with your stick – three times. Then we'll come in.

ARTHUR. You don't think that might look a trifle coincidental?

GRACE. Sh!

She disappears from view as the hall door opens and VIOLET *comes in.*

VIOLET. (*Announcing.*) Mr. Watherstone.

JOHN WATHERSTONE *comes in. He is a man of about thirty, dressed in an extremely well-cut morning coat and striped trousers, an attire which, though excused by church parade, we may well feel has been donned for this occasion.*

ARTHUR. How are you, John? I'm very glad to see you.

JOHN. How do you do, sir?

ARTHUR. Will you forgive me not getting up? My arthritis has been troubling me rather a lot, lately.

JOHN. I'm very sorry to hear that, sir. Catherine told me it was better.

ARTHUR. It was, for a time. Now it's worse again. Do you smoke? (*He indicates a cigarette-box.*)

JOHN. Yes, sir. I do. Thank you. (*He takes a cigarette, adding hastily.*) In moderation, of course.

ARTHUR. (*With a faint smile.*) Of course.

Pause, while JOHN *lights his cigarette and* ARTHUR *watches him.*

Well, now. I understand you wish to marry my daughter.

JOHN. Yes, sir. That's to say, I've proposed to her and she's done me the honour of accepting me.

ARTHUR. I see. I trust when you corrected yourself, your second statement wasn't a denial of your first? (JOHN *looks puzzled.*) I mean, you do *really* wish to marry her?

JOHN. Of course, sir.

ARTHUR. Why, of course? There are plenty of people about who don't wish to marry her.

JOHN. I mean, of course, because I proposed to her.

ARTHUR. That, too, doesn't necessarily follow. However, we don't need to quibble. We'll take the sentimental side of the project for granted. As regards the more practical aspect, perhaps you won't mind if I ask you a few rather personal questions?

JOHN. Naturally not, sir. It's your duty.

ARTHUR. Quite so. Now, your income. Are you able to live on it?

JOHN. No, sir. I'm in the regular army.

ARTHUR. Yes, of course.

JOHN. But my army pay is supplemented by an allowance from my father.

ARTHUR. So I understand. Now, your father's would be, I take it, about twenty-four pounds a month.

JOHN. Yes, sir, that's exactly right.

ARTHUR. So that your total income – with your subaltern's pay and allowances plus the allowance from your father, would be, I take it, about four hundred and twenty pounds a year?

JOHN. Again, exactly the figure.

ARTHUR. Well, well. It all seems perfectly satisfactory. I really don't think I need delay my congratulations any longer. (*He extends his hand, which* JOHN, *gratefully, takes.*)

JOHN. Thank you, sir, very much.

ARTHUR. I must say, it was very good of you to be so frank and informative.

JOHN. Not at all.

ARTHUR. Your answers to my questions deserve an equal
frankness from me about Catherine's own affairs. I'm afraid
she's not – just in case you thought otherwise – the daughter of
a rich man.

JOHN. I didn't think otherwise, sir.

ARTHUR. Good. Well, now –

*He suddenly cocks his head on one side and listens. There is the
sound of a gramophone playing 'Hitchy-koo' from somewhere
upstairs.*

Would you be so good as to touch the bell?

JOHN *does so*.

Thank you. Well, now, continuing about my own financial
affairs. The Westminster Bank pay me a small pension – three
hundred and fifty to be precise – and my wife has about two
hundred a year of her own. Apart from that we have nothing,
except such savings as I've been able to make during my career
at the bank. The interest from which raises my total income to
approximately eight hundred pounds per annum.

VIOLET *comes in*.

VIOLET. You rang, sir?

ARTHUR. Yes, Violet. My compliments to Mr. Dickie and if he
doesn't stop that cacophonous hullaballoo at once, I'll throw
him and his infernal machine into the street.

VIOLET. Yes, sir. What was that word again? Cac – something –

ARTHUR. Never mind. Say anything you like, only stop him.

VIOLET. Well, sir, I'll do my best, but you know what Master
Dickie's like with his blessed old ragtime.

ARTHUR. Yes, Violet, I do.

VIOLET. I could say you don't think it's quite right on a Sunday.

ARTHUR. (*Roaring*.) You can say I don't think it's quite right on
any day. Just stop him making that confounded din, that's all.

VIOLET. Yes, sir.

She goes out.

ARTHUR. (*Apologetically*.) Our Violet has no doubt already been
explained to you?

JOHN. I don't think so, sir. Is any explanation necessary?

ARTHUR. I fear it is. She came to us direct from an orphanage
when she was fourteen, as a sort of under-between-maid on
probation, and in that capacity she was quite satisfactory; but

I am afraid, as parlourmaid, she has developed certain marked eccentricities in the performance of her duties, due, no doubt, to the fact that she has never fully known what those duties were. Well, now, where were we? Ah, yes. I was telling you about my sources of income, was I not?

JOHN. Yes, sir.

ARTHUR. Now, in addition to the ordinary expenses of life, I have to maintain two sons – one at Osborne, and the other at Oxford – neither of whom, I'm afraid, will be in a position to support themselves for some time to come – one because of his extreme youth and the other because of – er – other reasons.

The gramophone stops suddenly.

So, you see, I am not in a position to be very lavish as regards Catherine's dowry.

JOHN. No, sir. I quite see that.

ARTHUR. I propose to settle on her one-sixth of my total capital, which, worked out to the final fraction, is exactly eight hundred and thirty-three pounds six shillings and eight pence. But let us deal in round figures and say eight hundred and fifty pounds.

JOHN. I call that very generous, sir.

ARTHUR. Not as generous as I would have liked, I'm afraid. However – as my wife would say – beggars can't be choosers.

JOHN. Exactly, sir.

ARTHUR. Well, then, if you're agreeable to that arrangement, I don't think there's anything more we need discuss.

JOHN. No, sir.

ARTHUR. Splendid.

Pause. ARTHUR takes his stick, and raps it, with an air of studied unconcern, three times on the floor. Nothing happens.

JOHN. Pretty rotten weather, isn't it?

ARTHUR. Yes. Vile.

He raps again. Again nothing happens.

Would you care for another cigarette?

JOHN. No, thank you, sir. I'm still smoking.

ARTHUR takes up his stick to rap again, and then thinks better of it. He goes slowly but firmly to the dining-room door, which he throws open.

ARTHUR. (*In apparent surprise.*) Well, imagine that! My wife and daughter are in here of all places. Come in, Grace. Come in, Catherine. John's here.

GRACE *comes in, with* CATHERINE *behind.*

GRACE. Why, John – how nice! (*She shakes hands.*) My, you do look a swell! Doesn't he, Kate, darling?

CATHERINE. Quite one of the Knuts.

Pause. GRACE *is unable to repress herself.*

GRACE. (*Coyly.*) Well?

ARTHUR. Well, what?

GRACE. How did your little talk go?

ARTHUR. (*Testily.*) I understood you weren't supposed to know we were having a little talk.

GRACE. Oh, you are infuriating! Is everything all right, John?

JOHN *nods, smiling.*

Oh, I'm so glad. I really am.

JOHN. Thank you, Mrs. Winslow.

GRACE. May I kiss you? After all, I'm practically your mother, now.

JOHN. Yes. Of course.

He allows himself to be kissed.

ARTHUR. While I, by the same token, am practically your father, but if you will forgive me –

JOHN. (*Smiling.*) Certainly, sir.

ARTHUR. Grace, I think we might allow ourselves a little modest celebration at luncheon. Will you find me the key of the cellars?

He goes out through the hall door.

GRACE. Yes, dear. (*She turns at the door. Coyly.*) I don't suppose you two will mind being left alone for a few minutes, will you?

She follows her husband out. JOHN *goes to* CATHERINE *and kisses her.*

CATHERINE. Was it an ordeal?

JOHN. I was scared to death.

CATHERINE. My poor darling –

JOHN. The annoying thing was that I had a whole lot of neatly turned phrases ready for him and he wouldn't let me use them.

CATHERINE. Such as?

JOHN. Oh – how proud and honoured I was by your acceptance of me, and how determined I was to make you a loyal and devoted husband – and to maintain you in the state to which you were accustomed – all that sort of thing. All very sincerely meant.

CATHERINE. Anything about loving me a little?

JOHN. (*Lightly.*) That I thought we could take for granted. So did your father, incidentally.

CATHERINE. I see. (*She gazes at him.*) Goodness, you do look smart!

JOHN. Not bad, is it? Poole's.

CATHERINE. What about *your* father? How did he take it?

JOHN. All right.

CATHERINE. I bet he didn't.

JOHN. Oh, yes. He's been wanting me to get married for years. Getting worried about grandchildren, I suppose.

CATHERINE. He disapproves of me, doesn't he?

JOHN. Oh, no. Whatever makes you think that?

CATHERINE. He has a way of looking at me through his monocle that shrivels me up.

JOHN. He's just being a colonel, darling, that's all. All colonels look at you like that. Anyway, what about the way your father looks at me! Tell me, are all your family as scared of him as I am?

CATHERINE. Dickie is, of course; and Ronnie, though he doesn't need to be. Father worships him. I don't know about Mother being scared of him. Sometimes, perhaps. I'm not – ever.

JOHN. You're not scared of anything, are you?

CATHERINE. Oh, yes. Heaps of things.

JOHN. Such as?

CATHERINE. (*With a smile.*) Oh – they're nearly all concerned with you.

RONNIE *looks cautiously in at the window door. He now presents a very bedraggled and woebegone appearance, with his uniform wringing wet, and his damp hair over his eyes.*

JOHN. You might be a little more explicit –

RONNIE. (*In a low voice.*) Kate!

CATHERINE *turns and sees him.*

CATHERINE. (*Amazed.*) Ronnie! What on earth –

RONNIE. Where's Father?

CATHERINE. I'll go and tell him –

RONNIE. (*Urgently.*) No, don't. Please, Kate, don't!

CATHERINE, *halfway to the door, stops, puzzled.*

CATHERINE. What's the trouble, Ronnie?

RONNIE, *trembling on the edge of tears, does not answer her. She approaches him.*

You're wet through. You'd better go and change.

RONNIE. No.

CATHERINE. (*Gently.*) What's the trouble, darling? You can tell me.

RONNIE *looks at* JOHN.

You know John Watherstone, Ronnie. You met him last holidays, don't you remember?

RONNIE *remains silent, obviously reluctant to talk in front of a comparative stranger.*

JOHN. (*Tactfully.*) I'll disappear.

CATHERINE. (*Pointing to dining-room.*) In there, do you mind?

JOHN *goes out quietly.* CATHERINE *gently leads* RONNIE *further into the room.*

Now, darling, tell me. What is it? Have you run away?

RONNIE *shakes his head, evidently not trusting himself to speak.*

What is it, then?

RONNIE *pulls out the document from his pocket which we have seen him reading in an earlier scene, and slowly hands it to her.* CATHERINE *reads it quietly.*

Oh, God!

RONNIE. I didn't do it.

CATHERINE *re-reads the letter in silence.*

RONNIE. Kate, I didn't. Really, I didn't.

CATHERINE. (*Abstractedly.*) No, darling. (*She seems uncertain what to do.*) This letter is addressed to Father. Did you open it?

RONNIE. Yes.

CATHERINE. You shouldn't have done that –

RONNIE. I was going to tear it up. Then I heard you come in from church and ran into the garden – I didn't know what to do –

CATHERINE. (*Still distracted.*) Did they send you up to London all by yourself?

RONNIE. They sent a petty officer up with me. He was supposed to wait and see Father, but I sent him away. (*Indicating letter.*) Kate – shall we tear it up, now?

CATHERINE. No, darling.

RONNIE. We could tell Father term had ended two days sooner –

CATHERINE. No, darling.

RONNIE. I didn't do it – really I didn't –

DICKIE *comes in from the hall. He does not seem surprised to see* RONNIE.

DICKIE. (*Cheerfully.*) Hullo, Ronnie, old lad. How's everything?

RONNIE *turns away from him.*

CATHERINE. You knew he was here?

DICKIE. Oh, yes. His trunks and things are all over our room. Trouble?

CATHERINE. Yes.

DICKIE. I'm sorry.

CATHERINE. You stay here with him. I'll find Mother.

DICKIE. All right.

CATHERINE *goes out by the hall door. There is a pause.*

DICKIE. What's up, old chap?

RONNIE. Nothing.

DICKIE. Come on – tell me.

RONNIE. It's all right.

DICKIE. Have you been sacked?

RONNIE *nods.*

Bad luck. What for?

RONNIE. I didn't do it!

DICKIE. (*Reassuringly.*) No, of course you didn't.

RONNIE. Honestly, I didn't.

DICKIE. That's all right, old chap. No need to go on about it. I believe you.

RONNIE. You don't.

DICKIE. Well, I don't know what it is they've sacked you for, yet –

RONNIE. (*In a low voice.*) Stealing.

DICKIE. (*Evidently relieved.*) Oh, is that all? Good Lord! I didn't know they sacked chaps for *that,* these days.

RONNIE. I didn't do it.

DICKIE. Why, good heavens, at school we used to pinch everything we could jolly well lay our hands on. All of us. I remember there was one chap – Carstairs his name was – captain of cricket, believe it or not – absolutely nothing was safe with him – nothing at all. Pinched a squash racket of mine once, I remember –

He has quietly approached RONNIE, *and now puts his arm on his shoulder.*

Believe me, old chap, pinching's nothing. Nothing at all. I say – you're a bit damp, aren't you?

RONNIE. I've been out in the rain –

DICKIE. You're shivering a bit, too, aren't you? Oughtn't you to go and change? I mean, we don't want you catching pneumonia –

RONNIE. I'm all right.

GRACE comes in, with CATHERINE following. GRACE comes quickly to RONNIE, who, as he sees her, turns away from DICKIE and runs into her arms.

GRACE. There, darling! It's all right, now.

RONNIE begins to cry quietly, his head buried in her dress.

RONNIE. (*His voice muffled.*) I didn't do it, Mother.

GRACE. No, darling. Of course you didn't. We'll go upstairs now, shall we, and get out of these nasty wet clothes.

RONNIE. Don't tell Father.

GRACE. No, darling. Not yet. I promise. Come along now.

She leads him towards the door held open by CATHERINE.

Your new uniform, too, What a shame!

She goes out with him.

DICKIE. I'd better go and keep 'cave' for them. Ward off the old man if he looks like going upstairs.

CATHERINE nods.

(*At door*.) I say – who's going to break the news to him eventually? I mean, someone'll have to.

CATHERINE. Don't let's worry about that now.

DICKIE. Well, you can count me out. In fact, I don't want to be within a thousand miles of that explosion.

He goes out. CATHERINE *comes to the dining-room door, which she opens, and calls 'John!'* JOHN *comes in.*

JOHN. Bad news?

CATHERINE *nods. She is plainly upset, and dabs her eyes with her handkerchief.*

That's rotten for you. I'm awfully sorry.

CATHERINE. (*Violently.*) How can people be so cruel!

JOHN. (*Uncomfortably.*) Expelled, I suppose?

He gets his answer from her silence, while she recovers herself.

CATHERINE. God, how little imagination some people have! Why should they torture a child of that age, John, darling? What's the point of it?

JOHN. What's he supposed to have done?

CATHERINE. Stolen some money.

JOHN. Oh.

CATHERINE. Ten days ago, it said in the letter. Why on earth didn't they let us know? Just think what that poor little creature has been going through these last ten days down there, entirely alone, without anyone to look after him, knowing what he had to face at the end of it! And then, finally, they send him up to London with a petty officer – is it any wonder he's nearly out of his mind?

JOHN. It does seem pretty heartless, I admit.

CATHERINE. Heartless? It's cold, calculated inhumanity. God, how I'd love to have that Commanding Officer here for just two minutes! I'd – I'd –

JOHN. (*Gently.*) Darling, it's quite natural you should feel angry about it, but you must remember, he's not really at school. He's in the Service.

CATHERINE. What difference does that make?

JOHN. Well, they have ways of doing things in the Service which may seem to an outsider horribly brutal – but at least they're always scrupulously fair. You can take it from me, that there must have been a very full inquiry before they'd take a step of this sort. What's more, if there's been a delay of ten days, it would only have been in order to give the boy a better chance to clear himself –

Pause. CATHERINE *is silent.*

I'm sorry, Catherine, darling. I'd have done better to keep my mouth shut.

CATHERINE. No. What you said was perfectly true –

JOHN. It was tactless of me to say it, though. I'm sorry.

CATHERINE. (*Lightly.*) That's all right.

JOHN. Forgive me?

He lays his arm on her shoulder.

CATHERINE. (*Taking his hand.*) Nothing to forgive.

JOHN. Believe me, I'm awfully sorry. (*After a pause.*) How will your father take it?

CATHERINE. (*Simply.*) It might kill him –

There is the sound of voices in the hall.

Oh, heavens! We've got Desmond to lunch. I'd forgotten –

JOHN. Who?

CATHERINE. Desmond Curry – our family solicitor. Oh, Lord! (*In a hasty whisper.*) Darling – be polite to him, won't you?

JOHN. Why? Am I usually so rude to your guests?

CATHERINE. No, but he doesn't know about us yet –

JOHN. Who does?

CATHERINE. (*Still in a whisper.*) Yes, but he's been in love with me for years – it's a family joke –

VIOLET *comes in.*

VIOLET. (*Announcing.*) Mr. Curry.

DESMOND CURRY *comes in. He is a man of about forty-five, with the figure of an athlete gone to seed. He has a mildly furtive manner, rather as if he had just absconded with his firm's petty cash, but hopes no one is going to be too angry about it.* JOHN, *when he sees him, cannot repress a faint smile at the thought of his loving* CATHERINE. VIOLET *has made her exit.*

CATHERINE. Hullo, Desmond. I don't think you know John Watherstone –

DESMOND. No – but, of course, I've heard a lot about him –

JOHN. How do you do?

He wipes the smile off his face, as he meets CATHERINE'S *glance. There is a pause.*

DESMOND. Well, well, well. I trust I'm not early.

CATHERINE. No. Dead on time, Desmond – as always.

DESMOND. Capital. Capital.

There is another pause, broken by CATHERINE *and* JOHN *both suddenly speaking at once.*

CATHERINE. ⎱ (*Simultaneously.*) Tell me, Desmond.
JOHN. ⎰   Pretty ghastly this rain –

JOHN. I'm so sorry –

CATHERINE. It's quite all right. I was only going to ask how you did in your cricket match yesterday, Desmond.

DESMOND. Not too well, I'm afraid. My shoulder's still giving me trouble –

There is another pause.

(*At length.*) Well, well. I hear I'm to congratulate you both –

CATHERINE. Desmond – you know?

DESMOND. Violet told me, just now – in the hall. Yes – I must congratulate you both.

CATHERINE. Thank you so much, Desmond.

JOHN. Thank you.

DESMOND. Of course, it's quite expected, I know. Quite expected. Still it was rather a surprise, hearing it like that – from Violet in the hall –

CATHERINE. We were going to tell you, Desmond dear. It was only official this morning, you know. In fact, you're the first person to hear it.

DESMOND. Am I? Am I, indeed? Well, I'm sure you'll both be very happy.

CATHERINE. ⎱ (*Murmuring together.*) Thank you, Desmond.
JOHN. ⎰   Thank you.

DESMOND. Only this morning? Fancy.

GRACE *comes in.*

GRACE. Hullo, Desmond, dear.

DESMOND. Hullo, Mrs. Winslow.

GRACE. (*To* CATHERINE.) I've got him to bed –

CATHERINE. Good.

DESMOND. Nobody ill, I hope?

GRACE. No, no. Nothing wrong at all –

> ARTHUR *comes in, with a bottle under his arm. He rings the bell.*

ARTHUR. Grace, when did we last have the cellars seen to?

GRACE. I can't remember, dear.

ARTHUR. Well, they're in a shocking condition. Hullo, Desmond. How are you? You're not looking well.

DESMOND. Am I not? I've strained my shoulder, you know –

ARTHUR. Well, why do you play these ridiculous games of yours? Resign yourself to the onrush of middle age, and abandon them, my dear Desmond.

DESMOND. Oh, I could never do that. Not give up cricket. Not altogether.

JOHN. (*Making conversation.*) Are you any relation of D. W. H. Curry who used to play for Middlesex?

DESMOND. (*Whose moment has come.*) I am D. W. H. Curry.

GRACE. Didn't you know we had a great man in the room?

JOHN. Gosh! Curry of Curry's match?

DESMOND. That's right.

JOHN. Hat trick against the Players in – what year was it?

DESMOND. 1895. At Lord's. Twenty-six overs, nine maidens, thirty-seven runs, eight wickets.

JOHN. Gosh! Do you know you used to be a schoolboy hero of mine?

DESMOND. Did I? Did I, indeed?

JOHN. Yes. I had a signed photograph of you.

DESMOND. Yes. I used to sign a lot once, for schoolboys, I remember.

ARTHUR. Only for schoolboys, Desmond?

DESMOND. I fear so – yes. Girls took no interest in cricket in those days.

JOHN. Gosh! D. W. H. Curry – in person. Well, I'd never have thought it.

DESMOND. (*Sadly.*) I know. Very few people would nowadays –

CATHERINE. (*Quickly.*) Oh, John didn't mean that, Desmond –

DESMOND. I fear he did. (*He moves his arm.*) This is the main trouble. Too much office work and too little exercise, I fear.

ARTHUR. Nonsense. Too much exercise and too little office work.

VIOLET *comes in, in response to a bell rung by* ARTHUR *some moments before.*

VIOLET. You rang, sir?

ARTHUR. Yes, Violet. Bring some glasses, would you?

VIOLET. Very good, sir.

She goes out.

ARTHUR. I thought we'd try a little of the Madeira before luncheon – we're celebrating, you know, Desmond –

GRACE *jogs his arm furtively, indicating* DESMOND.

(*Adding hastily.*) – my wife's fifty-fourth birthday –

GRACE. Arthur! Really!

CATHERINE. It's all right, Father. Desmond knows –

DESMOND. Yes, indeed. It's wonderful news, isn't it? I'll most gladly drink a toast to the – er – to the –

ARTHUR. (*Politely.*) Happy pair, I think, is the phrase that is eluding you –

DESMOND. Well, as a matter of fact, I was looking for something new to say –

ARTHUR. (*Murmuring.*) A forlorn quest, my dear Desmond.

GRACE. (*Protestingly.*) Arthur, really! You mustn't be so rude.

ARTHUR. I meant, naturally, that no one – with the possible exception of Voltaire – could find anything new to say about an engaged couple –

DICKIE *comes in.*

Ah, my dear Dickie – just in time for a glass of Madeira in celebration of Kate's engagement to John –

VIOLET *comes in with a tray of glasses.* ARTHUR *begins to pour out the wine.*

DICKIE. Oh, is that all finally spliced up now? Kate definitely being entered for the marriage stakes. Good egg!

ARTHUR. Quite so. I should have added just now – with the possible exception of Voltaire and Dickie Winslow. (*To* VIOLET.) Take these round, will you, Violet?

> VIOLET *goes first to* GRACE, *then to* CATHERINE, *then to* JOHN, DESMOND, DICKIE, *and finally* ARTHUR.

CATHERINE. Are we allowed to drink our own healths?

ARTHUR. I think it's permissible.

GRACE. No. It's bad luck.

JOHN. We defy augury. Don't we, Kate?

GRACE. You mustn't say that, John dear. I know. You can drink each other's healths. That's all right.

ARTHUR. Are my wife's superstitious terrors finally allayed? Good.

> *The drinks have now been handed round.*

ARTHUR. (*Toasting.*) Catherine and John!

> *All drink –* CATHERINE *and* JOHN *to each other.* VIOLET *lingers, smiling, in the doorway.*

> (*Seeing* VIOLET.) Ah, Violet. We mustn't leave you out. You must join this toast.

VIOLET. Well – thank you, sir.

> *He pours her out a glass.*

> Not too much, sir, please. Just a sip.

ARTHUR. Quite so. Your reluctance would be more convincing if I hadn't noticed you'd brought an extra glass –

VIOLET. (*Taking glass from* ARTHUR.) Oh, I didn't bring it for myself, sir. I brought it for Master Ronnie – (*She extends her glass.*) Miss Kate and Mr. John.

> *She takes a sip, makes a wry face, and hands the glass back to* ARTHUR.

ARTHUR. You brought an extra glass for Master Ronnie, Violet?

VIOLET. (*Mistaking his bewilderment.*) Well – I thought you might allow him just a sip, sir. Just to drink the toast. He's that grown up these days.

> *She turns to go. The others, with the exception of* DESMOND, *who is staring gloomily into his glass, are frozen with apprehension.*

ARTHUR. Master Ronnie isn't due back from Osborne until Tuesday, Violet.

VIOLET. (*Turning*.) Oh, no, sir. He's back already. Came back unexpected this morning, all by himself.

ARTHUR. No, Violet. That isn't true. Someone has been playing a joke –

VIOLET. Well, I saw him with my own two eyes, sir, as large as life, just before you come in from church – and then I heard Mrs. Winslow talking to him in his room –

ARTHUR. Grace – what does this mean?

CATHERINE. (*Instinctively taking charge*.) All right, Violet. You can go –

VIOLET. Yes, miss.

She goes out.

ARTHUR. (*To* CATHERINE.) Did *you* know Ronnie was back?

CATHERINE. Yes –

ARTHUR. And you, Dickie?

DICKIE. Yes, Father.

ARTHUR. Grace?

GRACE. (*Helplessly*.) We thought it best you shouldn't know – for the time being. Only for the time being, Arthur.

ARTHUR. (*Slowly*.) Is the boy very ill?

No one answers. ARTHUR *looks from one face to another in bewilderment.*

Answer me, someone! Is the boy very ill? Why must I be kept in the dark like this? Surely I have the right to know. If he's ill I must be with him –

CATHERINE. (*Steadily*.) No, Father. He's not ill.

ARTHUR *suddenly realizes the truth from her tone of voice.*

ARTHUR. Will someone tell me what has happened, please?

GRACE *looks at* CATHERINE *with helpless inquiry.*
CATHERINE *nods.* GRACE *takes a letter from her dress.*

GRACE. (*Timidly*.) He brought this letter for you – Arthur.

ARTHUR. Read it to me, please –

GRACE. Arthur – not in front of –

ARTHUR. Read it to me, please.

GRACE *again looks at* CATHERINE *for advice, and again receives a nod.* GRACE *begins to read.*

GRACE. (*Reading*.) 'Confidential. I am commanded by My Lords Commissioners of the Admiralty to inform you that they have received a communication from the Commanding Officer of the Royal Naval College at Osborne, reporting the theft of a five-shilling postal order at the College on the 7th instant, which was afterwards cashed at the Post Office. Investigation of the circumstances of the case leaves no other conclusion possible than that the postal order was taken by your son, Cadet Ronald Arthur Winslow. My Lords deeply regret that they must therefore request you to withdraw your son from the College.' It's signed by someone – I can't quite read his name –

She turns away quickly to hide her tears. CATHERINE *puts a comforting arm on her shoulder.* ARTHUR *has not changed his attitude. There is a pause, during which we can hear the sound of a gong in the hall outside.*

ARTHUR. (*At length*.) Desmond – be so good as to call Violet.

DESMOND *does so. There is another pause, until* VIOLET *comes in.*

VIOLET. Yes, sir.

ARTHUR. Violet, will you ask Master Ronnie to come down and see me, please?

GRACE. Arthur – he's in bed.

ARTHUR. You told me he wasn't ill.

GRACE. He's not at all well.

ARTHUR. Do as I say, please, Violet.

VIOLET. Very good, sir.

She goes out.

ARTHUR. Perhaps the rest of you would go in to luncheon? Grace, would you take them in?

GRACE. (*Hovering*.) Arthur – don't you think –

ARTHUR. (*Ignoring her.*) Dickie, will you decant that bottle of claret I brought up from the cellar? I put it on the sideboard in the dining-room.

DICKIE. Yes, Father.

He goes out.

ARTHUR. Will you go in, Desmond? And John?

The two men go out into the dining-room, in silence. GRACE *still hovers.*

GRACE. Arthur?

ARTHUR. Yes, Grace?

GRACE. Please don't – please don't – (*She stops, uncertainly.*)

ARTHUR. What mustn't I do?

GRACE. Please don't forget he's only a child –

ARTHUR does not answer her. CATHERINE takes her mother's arm.

CATHERINE. Come on, Mother.

She leads her mother to the dining-room door. At the door GRACE looks back at ARTHUR. He has still not altered his position and is ignoring her. She goes into the dining-room, followed by CATHERINE. ARTHUR does not move after they are gone. After an appreciable pause there comes a timid knock on the door.

ARTHUR. Come in.

RONNIE appears in the doorway. He is in a dressing-gown. He stands on the threshold.

Come in and shut the door.

RONNIE closes the door behind him.

Come over here.

RONNIE walks slowly up to his father. ARTHUR gazes at him steadily for some time, without speaking.

(*At length.*) Why aren't you in your uniform?

RONNIE. (*Murmuring.*) It got wet.

ARTHUR. How did it get wet?

RONNIE. I was out in the garden in the rain.

ARTHUR. Why?

RONNIE. (*Reluctantly.*) I was hiding.

ARTHUR. From me?

RONNIE nods.

Do you remember once, you promised me that if ever you were in trouble of any sort you would come to me first?

RONNIE. Yes, Father.

ARTHUR. Why didn't you come to me now? Why did you have to go and hide in the garden?

RONNIE. I don't know, Father.

ARTHUR. Are you so frightened of me?

RONNIE *does not reply.* ARTHUR *gazes at him for a moment, then picks up the letter.*

In this letter it says you stole a postal order.

RONNIE *opens his mouth to speak.* ARTHUR *stops him.*

Now, I don't want you to say a word until you've heard what *I've* got to say. If you did it, you must tell me. I shan't be angry with you, Ronnie – provided you tell me the truth. But if you tell me a lie, I shall know it, because a lie between you and me can't be hidden. I shall know it, Ronnie – so remember that before you speak. (*Pause.*) Did you steal this postal order?

RONNIE. (*Without hesitation.*) No, Father. I didn't.

ARTHUR. (*Staring into his eyes.*) Did you steal this postal order?

RONNIE. No, Father. I didn't.

ARTHUR *continues to stare into his eyes for a second, then relaxes and pushes him gently away.*

ARTHUR. Go on back to bed.

RONNIE *goes gratefully to the door.*

And in future I trust that a son of mine will at least show enough sense to come in out of the rain.

RONNIE. Yes, Father.

He disappears. ARTHUR *gets up quite briskly and goes to the telephone in the corner of the room.*

ARTHUR. (*At telephone.*) Hullo. Are you there? (*Speaking very distinctly.*) I want to put a trunk call through, please. A trunk call ... Yes ... The Royal Naval College, Osborne ... That's right ... Replace receiver? Certainly.

He replaces receiver and then, after a moment's meditation, turns and walks briskly into the dining-room.

Curtain

Act Two

Scene: the same, nine months later. It is about six o'clock, of a spring evening.

DICKIE *is winding up his gramophone which, somehow or other, appears to have found its way back into the drawing-room. A pile of books and an opened notebook on the table provide evidence of interrupted labours.*

The gramophone, once started, emits a scratchy and muffled rendering of an early ragtime. DICKIE *listens for a few seconds with evident appreciation, then essays a little* pas seul.

CATHERINE *comes in. She is in evening dress.* DICKIE *switches off gramophone.*

DICKIE. Hullo. Do you think the old man can hear this upstairs?

CATHERINE. I shouldn't think so. I couldn't.

DICKIE. Soft needle and an old sweater down the horn. Is the doctor still with him?

CATHERINE *nods.*

What's the verdict, do you know?

CATHERINE. I heard him say Father needed a complete rest.

DICKIE. Don't we all.

CATHERINE. (*Indicating books.*) It doesn't look as if you did. He said he ought to go to the country and forget all his worries –

DICKIE. Fat chance there is of that, I'd say.

CATHERINE. I know.

DICKIE. I say, you look a treat. New dress?

CATHERINE. Is it likely? No, it's an old one I've had done up.

DICKIE. Where are you going to?

CATHERINE. Daly's. Dinner first – at the Cri.

DICKIE. Nice. You wouldn't care to take me along with you, I suppose?

CATHERINE. You suppose quite correctly.

DICKIE. John wouldn't mind.

CATHERINE. I dare say not. I would.

DICKIE. I wish I had someone to take me out. In your new feminist world do you suppose women will be allowed to do some of the paying?

CATHERINE. Certainly.

DICKIE. Really? Then the next time you're looking for someone to chain themselves to Mr. Asquith you can jolly well call on me –

CATHERINE. (*Laughing*.) Edwina might take you out if you gave her the hint. She's very rich –

DICKIE. If I gave Edwina a hint of that sort I wouldn't see her this side of doomsday.

CATHERINE. You sound a little bitter, Dickie dear.

DICKIE. Oh, no. Not bitter. Just realistic.

VIOLET *comes in with an evening paper on a salver.*

DICKIE. Good egg! The *Star!*

CATHERINE *makes a grab for it and gets it before* DICKIE.

VIOLET. You won't throw it away, will you, miss? If there's anything in it again, cook and I would like to read it, after you.

CATHERINE *is hastily turning over the pages, with* DICKIE *craning his head over her shoulder.*

CATHERINE. No. That's all right, Violet.

VIOLET *goes out.*

Here it is. (*Reading*.) 'The Osborne cadet.' There are two more letters. (*Reading*.) ' Sir. I am entirely in agreement with your correspondent, Democrat, concerning the scandalously high-handed treatment by the Admiralty of the case of the Osborne Cadet. The efforts of Mr. Arthur Winslow to secure a fair trial for his son have evidently been thwarted at every turn by a soulless oligarchy' –

DICKIE. Soulless oligarchy. That's rather good –

CATHERINE. – 'it is high time private and peaceful citizens of this country awoke to the increasing encroachment of their ancient freedom by the new despotism of Whitehall. The Englishman's home was once said to be his castle. It seems it is rapidly becoming his prison. Your obedient servant, *Libertatis Amator.'*

DICKIE. Good for old Amator!

CATHERINE. The other's from Perplexed. (*Reading*.) 'Dear Sir. I cannot understand what all the fuss is about in the case of the Osborne Cadet. Surely we have more important matters to get ourselves worked up about than a fourteen-year-old boy and a five-shilling postal order.' Silly old fool!

DICKIE. How do you know he's old?

CATHERINE. Isn't it obvious? (*Reading.*) 'With the present troubles in the Balkans and a certain major European Power rapidly outbuilding our navy, the Admiralty might be forgiven if it stated that it had rather more urgent affairs to deal with than Master Ronnie Winslow's little troubles. A further inquiry before the Judge Advocate of the Fleet has now fully confirmed the original findings that the boy was guilty. I sincerely trust that this will finally end this ridiculous and sordid little storm in a teacup. I am, sir, etc., Perplexed.'

Pause.

DICKIE. (*Reading over her shoulder.*) 'This correspondence must now cease. – Editor.' Damn!

CATHERINE. Oh, dear! How hopeless it seems, sometimes.

DICKIE. Yes, it does, doesn't it? (*Thoughtfully, after a pause.*) You know, Kate – don't give me away to the old man, will you – but the awful thing is, if it hadn't been my own brother, I think I might quite likely have seen Perplexed's point.

CATHERINE. Might you?

DICKIE. Well, I mean – looking at it from every angle and all that – it does seem rather a much ado about damn all. I mean to say – a mere matter of pinching. (*Bitterly.*) And it's all so beastly expensive. Let's cheer ourselves up with some music. (*He sets machine going.*)

CATHERINE. (*Listening to the record.*) Is that what it's called?

DICKIE. Come and practise a few steps.

CATHERINE *joins him and they dance, in the manner of the period, with arms fully outstretched and working up and down, pump-handle style.*

(*Surprised.*) I say! Jolly good!

CATHERINE. Thank you, Dickie.

DICKIE. Who taught you? John, I suppose.

CATHERINE. No. I taught John, as it happens –

DICKIE. Feminism – even in love?

CATHERINE *nods, smiling. Pause, while they continue to dance.*

When's the happy date now?

CATHERINE. Postponed again.

DICKIE. Oh, no. Why?

CATHERINE. His father's gone abroad for six months.

DICKIE. Why pay any attention to that old – (*He substitutes the word*.) – gentleman?

CATHERINE. I wouldn't – but John does – so I have to.

Something in her tone makes DICKIE *stop dancing and gaze at her seriously.*

DICKIE. I say – nothing wrong, is there?

CATHERINE *shakes her head, smiling, but not too emphatically.*

I mean – you're not going to be left on the altar rails or anything, are you?

CATHERINE. Oh, no. I'll get him past the altar rails, if I have to drag him there.

DICKIE. (*As they resume their dance*.) Do you think you might have to?

CATHERINE. Quite frankly, yes.

DICKIE. Competition?

CATHERINE. Not yet. Only – differences of opinion.

DICKIE. I see. Well, take some advice from an old hand, will you?

CATHERINE. Yes, Dickie.

DICKIE. Suppress your opinions. Men don't like 'em in their lady friends, even if they agree with 'em. And if they don't – it's fatal. Pretend to be half-witted, like Edwina, then he'll adore you.

CATHERINE. I know. I do, sometimes, and then I forget. Still, you needn't worry. If there's ever a clash between what I believe and what I feel, there's not much doubt about which will win.

DICKIE. That's the girl. Of course, I don't know why you didn't fall in love with Ramsay MacDonald –

ARTHUR *comes in. He is walking with more difficulty than when we last saw him.* DICKIE *and* CATHERINE *hastily stop dancing, and* DICKIE *turns off the gramophone.*

CATHERINE. (*Quickly.*) It was entirely my fault, Father. I enticed Dickie from his work to show me a few dance steps.

ARTHUR. Oh? I must admit I am surprised you succeeded.

DICKIE. (*Getting off the subject.*) What did the doctor say, Father?

ARTHUR. He said, if I remember his exact words, that we weren't quite as well as when we last saw each other. That information seems expensive at a guinea. (*Seeing the evening paper.*) Oh, is that the *Star?* Let me see it, please.

CATHERINE *brings it over to him.*

John will be calling for you here, I take it?

CATHERINE. Yes, Father.

ARTHUR. It might be better, perhaps, if you didn't ask him in. This room will shortly be a clutter of journalists, solicitors, barristers, and other impedimenta.

CATHERINE. Is Sir Robert Morton coming to see you here?

ARTHUR. (*Deep in the* Star.) I could hardly go and see him, could I?

DICKIE, *in deference to his father's presence, has returned to his books.* ARTHUR *reads the* Star. CATHERINE *glances at herself in the mirror, and then wanders to the door.*

CATHERINE. I must go and do something about my hair.

DICKIE. What's the matter with your hair?

CATHERINE. Nothing, except I don't like it very much.

She goes out. DICKIE *opens two more books with a busy air and chews his pencil.* ARTHUR *finishes reading the* Star *and stares moodily into space.*

ARTHUR. (*At length.*) I wonder if I could sue "Perplexed".

DICKIE. It might be a way of getting the case into court.

ARTHUR. On the other hand, he has not been libellous. Merely base.

He throws the paper away and regards DICKIE *thoughtfully.* DICKIE, *feeling his father's eye on him, is elaborately industrious.*

ARTHUR. (*At length, politely.*) Do you mind if I disturb you for a moment?

DICKIE. (*Pushing books away.*) No, Father.

ARTHUR. I want to ask you a question. But before I do I must impress on you the urgent necessity for an absolutely truthful answer.

DICKIE. Naturally.

ARTHUR. Naturally means by nature, and I'm afraid I have not yet noticed that it has invariably been your nature to answer my questions truthfully.

DICKIE. Oh. Well, I will, this one, Father, I promise.

ARTHUR. Very well. (*He stares at him for a moment.*) What do you suppose one of your bookmaker friends would lay in the way of odds against your getting a degree?

Pause.

DICKIE. Oh. Well, let's think. Say – about evens.

ARTHUR. Hm. I rather doubt if at that price your friend would find many takers.

DICKIE. Well – perhaps seven to four against.

ARTHUR. I see. And what about the odds against your eventually becoming a Civil Servant?

DICKIE. Well – a bit steeper, I suppose.

ARTHUR. Exactly. Quite a bit steeper.

Pause.

DICKIE. You don't want to have a bet, do you?

ARTHUR. No, Dickie. I'm not a gambler. And that's exactly the trouble. Unhappily I'm no longer in a position to gamble two hundred pounds a year on what you yourself admit is an outside chance.

DICKIE. Not an outside chance, Father. A good chance.

ARTHUR. Not good enough, Dickie, I'm afraid – with things as they are at the moment. Definitely not good enough. I fear my mind is finally made up.

There is a long pause.

DICKIE. You want me to leave Oxford – is that it?

ARTHUR. I'm very much afraid so, Dickie.

DICKIE. Oh. Straight away?

ARTHUR. No. You can finish your second year.

DICKIE. And what then?

ARTHUR. I can get you a job in the bank.

DICKIE. (*Quietly.*) Oh, Lord!

Pause.

ARTHUR. (*Rather apologetically.*) It'll be quite a good job, you know. Luckily my influence in the bank still counts for something.

DICKIE *gets up and wanders about, slightly in a daze.*

DICKIE. Father – if I promised you – I mean, *really* promised you – that from now on I'll work like a black –

ARTHUR *shakes his head slowly.*

It's the case, I suppose?

ARTHUR. It's costing me a lot of money.

DICKIE. I know. It must be. Still, couldn't you – I mean, isn't there any way –

ARTHUR *again shakes his head.*

Oh, Lord!

ARTHUR. I'm afraid this is rather a shock for you. I'm sorry.

DICKIE. What? No. No, it isn't, really. I've been rather expecting it, as a matter of fact – especially since I've heard you are hoping to brief Sir Robert Morton. Still, I can't say but what it isn't a bit of a slap in the face.

There is a ring at the front door.

ARTHUR. There is a journalist coming to see me. Do you mind if we talk about this some other time?

DICKIE. No. Of course not, Father.

DICKIE *begins forlornly to gather his books.*

ARTHUR. (*With a half-smile.*) I should leave those there, if I were you.

DICKIE. Yes. I will. Good idea.

He goes to the door.

ARTHUR. (*Politely.*) Tell me – how is your nice friend, Miss Edwina Gunn, these days?

DICKIE. Very well, thanks awfully.

ARTHUR. You don't suppose she'd mind if you took her to the theatre – or gave her a little present perhaps?

DICKIE. Oh, I'm sure she wouldn't.

ARTHUR. I'm afraid I can only make it a couple of sovereigns.

ARTHUR *has taken out his sovereign case and now extracts two sovereigns.* DICKIE *comes and takes them.*

DICKIE. Thanks awfully, Father.

ARTHUR. With what's left over you can always buy something for yourself.

DICKIE. Oh. Well, as a matter of fact, I don't suppose there will be an awful lot left over. Still, it's jolly decent of you – I say, Father – I think I could do with a little spot of something. Would you mind?

ARTHUR. Of course not. You'll find the decanter in the dining-room.

DICKIE. Thanks awfully.

He goes to dining-room door.

ARTHUR. I must thank you, Dickie, for bearing what must have been a very unpleasant blow with some fortitude.

DICKIE. (*Uncomfortably.*) Oh. Rot, Father.

He goes out. ARTHUR *sighs deeply.* VIOLET *comes in at the hall door.*

VIOLET. (*Announcing proudly.*) The *Daily News!*

MISS BARNES *comes in. She is a rather untidily dressed woman of about forty with a gushing manner.*

MISS BARNES. Mr. Winslow? So good of you to see me.

ARTHUR. How do you do?

MISS BARNES. (*Simpering.*) You're surprised to see a lady reporter? I know. Everyone is. And yet why not? What could be more natural?

ARTHUR. What indeed? Pray sit down –

MISS BARNES. My paper usually sends me out on stories which have a special appeal to women – stories with a little heart, you know, like this one – a father's fight for his little boy's honour –

ARTHUR *visibly winces.*

ARTHUR. I venture to think this case has rather wider implications than that –

MISS BARNES. Oh, yes. The political angle. I know. Very interesting but not *quite* my line of country. Now, what I'd really like to do – is to get a nice picture of you and your little boy together. I've brought my assistant and camera. They're in the hall. Where is your little boy?

ARTHUR. My son is arriving from school in a few minutes. His mother has gone to the station to meet him.

MISS BARNES. (*Making a note.*) From school? How interesting. So you got a school to take him? I mean, they didn't mind the unpleasantness?

ARTHUR. No.

MISS BARNES. And why is he coming back this time?

ARTHUR. He hasn't been expelled again, if that is what you're implying. He is coming to London to be examined by Sir Robert Morton, whom we are hoping to brief –

MISS BARNES. Sir Robert Morton! (*She whistles appreciatively.*) Well!

ARTHUR. Exactly.

MISS BARNES. (*Doubtingly.*) But do you *really* think he'll take a little case like this?

ARTHUR. (*Explosively.*) It is *not* a little case, madam –

MISS BARNES. No, no. Of course not. But still – Sir Robert Morton!

ARTHUR. I understand that he is the best advocate in the country. He is certainly the most expensive –

MISS BARNES. Oh, yes. I suppose if one is prepared to pay his fee one can get him for almost *any* case.

ARTHUR. Once more, madam – this is *not* almost any case –

MISS BARNES. No, no. Of course not. Well, now, perhaps you wouldn't mind giving me a few details. When did it all start?

ARTHUR. Nine months ago. The first I knew of the charge was when my son arrived home with a letter from the Admiralty informing me of his expulsion. I telephoned Osborne to protest and was referred by them to the Lords of the Admiralty. My solicitors then took the matter up, and demanded from the Admiralty the fullest possible inquiry. For weeks we were ignored, then met with a blank refusal, and only finally got reluctant permission to view the evidence.

MISS BARNES. (*Indifferently.*) Really?

ARTHUR. My solicitors decided that the evidence was highly unsatisfactory, and fully justified the re-opening of proceedings. We applied to the Admiralty for a Court Martial. They ignored us. We applied for a civil trial. They ignored us again.

MISS BARNES. They ignored you?

ARTHUR. Yes. But after tremendous pressure had been brought to bear – letters to the papers, questions in the House, and other means open to private citizens of this country – the Admiralty eventually agreed to what they called an independent inquiry.

MISS BARNES. (*Vaguely.*) Oh, good!

ARTHUR. It was not good, madam. At that independent inquiry, conducted by the Judge Advocate of the Fleet – against whom

I am saying nothing, mind you – my son, – a child of fourteen, was not represented by counsel, solicitors, or friends. What do you think of that?

MISS BARNES. Fancy!

ARTHUR. You may well say fancy.

MISS BARNES. And what happened at the inquiry?

ARTHUR. What do you think happened? Inevitably he was found guilty again, and thus branded for the second time before the world as a thief and a forger –

MISS BARNES. (*Her attention wandering.*) What a shame!

ARTHUR. I need hardly tell you, madam, that I am not prepared to let the matter rest there. I shall continue to fight this monstrous injustice with every weapon and every means at my disposal. Now, it happens I have a plan –

MISS BARNES. Oh, what charming curtains! What are they made of? (*She rises and goes to window.*)

ARTHUR *sits for a moment in paralysed silence.*

ARTHUR (*At last.*) Madam – I fear I have no idea.

There is the sound of voices in the hall.

MISS BARNES. Ah. Do I hear the poor little chap himself?

The hall door opens and RONNIE *comes in boisterously, followed by* GRACE. *He is evidently in the highest of spirits.*

RONNIE. Hullo, Father! (*He runs to him.*)

ARTHUR. Hullo. Ronnie.

RONNIE. I say, Father! Mr. Moore says I'm to tell you I needn't come back until Monday if you like. So that gives me three whole days.

ARTHUR. Mind my leg!

RONNIE. Sorry, Father.

ARTHUR. How are you, my boy?

RONNIE. Oh, I'm absolutely tophole, Father. Mother says I've grown an inch –

MISS BARNES. Ah! Now that's exactly the way I'd like to take my picture. Would you hold it, Mr. Winslow? (*She goes to hall door and calls.*) Fred! Come in now, will you?

RONNIE. (*In a sibilant whisper.*) Who's she?

FRED *appears. He is a listless photographer, complete with apparatus.*

FRED. (*Gloomily.*) Afternoon, all.

MISS BARNES. That's the pose I suggest.

FRED. Yes. It'll do.

> *He begins to set up his apparatus.* ARTHUR, *holding* RONNIE *close against him in the pose suggested, turns his head to* GRACE.

ARTHUR. Grace, dear, this lady is from the *Daily News*. She is extremely interested in your curtains.

GRACE. (*Delighted.*) Oh, really! How nice!

MISS BARNES. Yes, indeed. I was wondering what they were made of.

GRACE. Well, it's an entirely new material, you know. I'm afraid I don't know what it's called, but I got them at Barkers last year. Apparently it's a sort of mixture of wild silk and –

MISS BARNES. (*Now genuinely busy with her pencil and pad.*) Just a second, Mrs. Winslow. I'm afraid my shorthand isn't very good. I must just get that down –

RONNIE. (*To* ARTHUR.) Father, are we going to be in the *Daily News?*

ARTHUR. It appears so –

RONNIE. Oh, good! They get the *Daily News* in the school library and everyone's bound to see it –

FRED. Quite still, please –

> *He takes his photograph.*

> All right, Miss Barnes. (*He goes out.*)

MISS BARNES. (*Engrossed with* GRACE.) Thank you, Fred. (*To* ARTHUR.) Goodbye, Mr. Winslow, and the very best of good fortune in your inspiring fight. (*Turning to* RONNIE.) Goodbye, little chap. Remember, the darkest hour is just before the dawn. Well, it was very good of you to tell me all that, Mrs. Winslow. I'm sure our readers will be most interested.

> GRACE *shows her out.*

RONNIE. What's she talking about?

ARTHUR. The case, I imagine.

RONNIE. Oh, the case. Father, do you know the train had fourteen coaches?

ARTHUR. Did it indeed?

RONNIE. Yes. All corridor.

ARTHUR. Remarkable.

RONNIE. Of course, it was one of the very biggest expresses. I walked all the way down it from one end to the other.

ARTHUR. I had your half-term report, Ronnie.

RONNIE. (*Suddenly silenced by perturbation.*) Oh, yes?

ARTHUR. On the whole it was pretty fair.

RONNIE. Oh, good.

ARTHUR. I'm glad you seem to be settling down so well. Very glad indeed.

GRACE *comes in.*

GRACE. What a charming woman, Arthur!

ARTHUR. Charming. I trust you gave her full details about our curtains?

GRACE. Oh, yes. I told her everything.

ARTHUR. (*Wearily.*) I'm so glad.

GRACE. I do think women reporters are a good idea –

RONNIE. (*Excitedly.*) I say, Father, will it be all right for me to stay still Monday? I mean, I won't be missing any work – only Divinity – (*He jogs his father's leg again.*)

ARTHUR. Mind my leg!

RONNIE. Oh, sorry, Father. Is it bad?

ARTHUR. Yes, it is. (*To* GRACE.) Grace, take him upstairs and get him washed. Sir Robert will be here in a few minutes.

GRACE. (*To* RONNIE.) Come on, darling.

RONNIE. All right. (*On his way to the door with his mother.*) I say, do you know how long the train took? 123 miles in two hours and fifty-two minutes. That's an average of 46.73 recurring miles an hour – I worked it out. Violet! Violet! I'm back.

He disappears, still chattering shrilly. GRACE *stops at the door.*

GRACE. Did the doctor say anything, dear?

ARTHUR. A great deal; but very little to the purpose.

GRACE. Violet says he left an ointment for your back. Four massages a day. Is that right?

ARTHUR. Something of the kind.

GRACE. I think you had better have one now, hadn't you, Arthur?

ARTHUR. No.

GRACE. But, dear, you've got plenty of time before Sir Robert comes, and if you don't have one now, you won't be able to have another before you go to bed.

ARTHUR. Precisely.

GRACE. But really, Arthur, it does seem awfully silly to spend all this money on doctors if you're not even going to do what they say.

ARTHUR. (*Impatiently.*) All right, Grace. All right. All right.

GRACE. Thank you, dear.

CATHERINE *comes in*.

CATHERINE. Ronnie's back, judging by the noise –

GRACE. (*Examining her.*) I must say that old frock has come out very well. John'll never know it isn't brand new –

CATHERINE. He's late, curse him.

ARTHUR. Grace, go on up and attend to Ronnie, and prepare the witch's brew for me. I'll come up when you are ready.

GRACE. Very well, dear. (*To* CATHERINE.) Yes, that does look good. I must say Mme Dupont's a treasure.

She goes out.

ARTHUR. (*Wearily.*) Oh, Kate, Kate! Are we both mad, you and I?

CATHERINE. What's the matter, Father?

ARTHUR. I don't know. I suddenly feel suicidally inclined. (*Bitterly.*) A father's fight for his little boy's honour. Special appeal to all women. Photo inset of Mrs. Winslow's curtains! Is there any hope for the world?

CATHERINE. (*Smiling.*) I think so, Father.

ARTHUR. Shall we drop the whole thing, Kate?

CATHERINE. I don't consider that a serious question, Father.

ARTHUR. (*Slowly.*) You realize that, if we go on, your marriage settlement must go?

CATHERINE. (*Lightly.*) Oh, yes. I gave that up for lost weeks ago.

ARTHUR. Things are all right between you and John, aren't they?

CATHERINE. Oh, yes, Father, of course. Everything's perfect.

ARTHUR. I mean – it won't make any difference between you, will it?

CATHERINE. Good heavens, no!

ARTHUR. Very well, then. Let us pin our faith to Sir Robert Morton.

CATHERINE is silent. ARTHUR looks at her as if he had expected an answer, then nods.

I see I'm speaking only for myself in saying that.

CATHERINE. (*Lightly.*) You know what I think of Sir Robert Morton, Father. Don't let's go into it again, now. It's too late, anyway.

ARTHUR. It's not too late. He hasn't accepted the brief yet.

CATHERINE. (*Shortly.*) Then I'm rather afraid I hope he never does. And that has nothing to do with my marriage settlement either.

Pause. ARTHUR looks angry for a second, then subsides.

ARTHUR. (*Mildly.*) I made inquiries about that fellow you suggested – I am told he is not nearly as good an advocate as Morton –

CATHERINE. He's not nearly so fashionable.

ARTHUR. (*Doubtfully.*) I want the best –

CATHERINE. The best in this case certainly isn't Morton.

ARTHUR. Then why does everyone say he is?

CATHERINE. (*Roused.*) Because if one happens to be a large monopoly attacking a Trade Union or a Tory paper libelling a Labour Leader, he *is* the best. But it utterly defeats me how you or anyone else could expect a man of his record to have even a tenth of his heart in a case where the boot is entirely on the other foot –

ARTHUR. Well, I imagine, if his heart isn't in it, he won't accept the brief.

CATHERINE. He might still. It depends what there is in it for him. Luckily there isn't much –

ARTHUR. (*Bitterly.*) There is a fairly substantial cheque –

CATHERINE. He doesn't want money. He must be a very rich man.

ARTHUR. What does he want, then?

CATHERINE. Anything that advances his interests.

ARTHUR shrugs his shoulders. Pause.

ARTHUR. I believe you are prejudiced because he spoke against woman's suffrage.

CATHERINE. I am. I'm prejudiced because he is always speaking against what is right and just. Did you read his speech in the House on the Trades Disputes Bill?

GRACE. (*Calling off.*) Arthur! Arthur!

ARTHUR. (*Smiling.*) Oh, well – in the words of the Prime Minister – let us wait and see.

He turns at the door.

You're my only ally, Kate. Without you I believe I should have given up long ago.

CATHERINE. Rubbish.

ARTHUR. It's true. Still, you must sometimes allow me to make my own decisions. I have an instinct about Morton.

CATHERINE does not reply.

(*Doubtfully.*) We'll see which is right – my instinct or your reason, eh?

He goes out.

CATHERINE. (*Half to herself.*) I'm afraid we will.

DICKIE comes out of the dining-room door.

DICKIE. (*Bitterly.*) Hullo, Kate.

CATHERINE. Hullo, Dickie.

DICKIE crosses mournfully to the other door.

What's the matter? Edwina jilted you or something?

DICKIE. Haven't you heard?

CATHERINE shakes her head.

I'm being scratched from the Oxford Stakes at the end of the year –

CATHERINE. Oh, Dickie! I'm awfully sorry –

DICKIE. Did you know it was in the wind?

CATHERINE. I knew there was a risk –

DICKIE. You might have warned a fellow. I fell plumb into the old man's trap. My gosh, I could just about murder that little brother of mine. (*Bitterly.*) What's he have to go about pinching postal orders for? And why the hell does he have to get himself nabbed doing it? Silly little blighter!

*He goes out gloomily. There is a ring at the front-door.
CATHERINE, obviously believing it is JOHN, picks up her cloak and goes to the hall door.*

CATHERINE. (*Calling.*) All right, Violet. It's only Mr. Watherstone. I'll answer it.

She goes out. There is the sound of voices in the hall, and then CATHERINE *reappears, leading in* DESMOND *and* SIR ROBERT MORTON. SIR ROBERT *is a man in the early forties, cadaverous and immensely elegant. He wears a long overcoat, and carries his hat and stick. He looks rather a fop, and his supercilious expression bears out this view.*

(*As she re-enters.*) I'm so sorry. I was expecting a friend. Won't you sit down, Sir Robert! My father won't be long.

SIR ROBERT *bows slightly, and sits down on a hard chair, still in his overcoat.*

Won't you sit here? It's far more comfortable.

SIR ROBERT. No, thank you.

DESMOND. (*Fussing.*) Sir Robert has a most important dinner engagement, so we came a little early.

CATHERINE. I see.

DESMOND. I'm afraid he can only spare us a very few minutes of his most valuable time this evening. Of course, it's a long way for him to come – so far from his chambers – and very good of him to do it, too, if I may say so –

He bows to SIR ROBERT, *who bows slightly back.*

CATHERINE. I know. I can assure you we're very conscious of it.

SIR ROBERT *gives her a quick look, and a faint smile.*

DESMOND. Perhaps I had better advise your father of our presence –

CATHERINE. Yes, do, Desmond. You'll find him in his bedroom – having his back rubbed.

DESMOND. Oh. I see.

He goes out. There is a pause.

CATHERINE. Is there anything I can get you, Sir Robert? A whisky and soda or a brandy?

SIR ROBERT. No, thank you.

CATHERINE. Will you smoke?

SIR ROBERT. No, thank you.

CATHERINE. (*Holding her cigarette.*) I hope you don't mind me smoking?

SIR ROBERT. Why should I?

CATHERINE. Some people find it shocking.

SIR ROBERT. (*Indifferently.*) A lady in her own home is surely entitled to behave as she wishes.

Pause.

CATHERINE. Won't you take your coat off, Sir Robert?

SIR ROBERT. No, thank you.

CATHERINE. You find it cold in here? I'm sorry.

SIR ROBERT. It's perfectly all right.

Conversation languishes again. SIR ROBERT *looks at his watch.*

CATHERINE. What time are you dining?

SIR ROBERT. Eight o'clock.

CATHERINE. Far from here?

SIR ROBERT. Devonshire House.

CATHERINE. Oh. Then of course you mustn't on any account be late.

SIR ROBERT. No.

There is another pause.

CATHERINE. I suppose you know the history of this case, do you, Sir Robert?

SIR ROBERT. (*Examining his nails.*) I believe I have seen most of the relevant documents.

CATHERINE. Do you think we can bring the case into Court by a collusive action?

SIR ROBERT. I really have no idea –

CATHERINE. Curry and Curry seem to think that might hold –

SIR ROBERT. Do they? They are a very reliable firm.

Pause. CATHERINE *is on the verge of losing her temper.*

CATHERINE. I'm rather surprised that a case of this sort should interest you, Sir Robert.

SIR ROBERT. Are you?

CATHERINE. It seems such a very trivial affair, compared to most of your great forensic triumphs.

SIR ROBERT, *staring languidly at the ceiling, does not reply.*

I was in Court during your cross-examination of Len Rogers, in the Trades Union embezzlement case.

SIR ROBERT. Really?

CATHERINE. It was masterly.

SIR ROBERT. Thank you.

CATHERINE. I suppose you heard that he committed suicide a few months ago?

SIR ROBERT. Yes. I had heard.

CATHERINE. Many people believed him innocent, you know.

SIR ROBERT. So I understand. (*After a faint pause*.) As it happens, however, he was guilty.

GRACE *comes in hastily.*

GRACE. Sir Robert? My husband's so sorry to have kept you, but he's just coming.

SIR ROBERT. It's perfectly all right. How do you do?

CATHERINE. Sir Robert is dining at Devonshire House, Mother.

GRACE. Oh, really? Oh, then you have to be punctual, of course, I do see that. It's the politeness of princes, isn't it?

SIR ROBERT. So they say.

GRACE. In this case the other way round, of course. Ah, I think I hear my husband on the stairs. I hope Catherine entertained you all right?

SIR ROBERT. (*With a faint bow to* CATHERINE.) Very well, thank you.

ARTHUR *comes in, followed by* DESMOND.

ARTHUR. Sir Robert? I am Arthur Winslow.

SIR ROBERT. How do you do?

ARTHUR. I understand you are rather pressed for time.

GRACE. Yes. He's dining at Devonshire House –

ARTHUR. Are you indeed? My son should be down in a minute. I expect you will wish to examine him.

SIR ROBERT. (*Indifferently*.) Just a few questions. I fear that is all I will have time for this evening –

ARTHUR. I am rather sorry to hear that. He has made the journey especially from school for this interview and I was hoping that by the end of it I should know definitely yes or no if you would accept the brief.

DESMOND. (*Pacifically*.) Well, perhaps Sir Robert would consent to finish his examination some other time?

SIR ROBERT. It might be arranged.

ARTHUR. Tomorrow?

SIR ROBERT. Tomorrow is impossible. I am in Court all the morning and in the House of Commons for the rest of the day. (*Carelessly.*) If a further examination should prove necessary it will have to be some time next week.

ARTHUR. I see. Will you forgive me if I sit down. (*He sits in his usual chair.*) Curry has been telling me you think it might be possible to proceed by Petition of Right.

CATHERINE. What's a Petition of Right?

DESMOND. Well – granting the assumption that the Admiralty, as the Crown, can do no wrong –

CATHERINE. (*Murmuring.*) I thought that was exactly the assumption we refused to grant.

DESMOND. In law, I mean. Now, a subject can sue the Crown, nevertheless, by Petition of Right, redress being granted as a matter of grace – and the custom is for the Attorney General – on behalf of the King – to endorse the Petition, and allow the case to come to Court.

SIR ROBERT. It is interesting to note that the exact words he uses on such occasions are: Let Right be done.

ARTHUR. Let Right be done? I like that phrase, sir.

SIR ROBERT. It has a certain ring about it – has it not? (*Languidly.*) Let Right be done.

RONNIE *comes in. He is in an Eton suit, looking very spick and span.*

ARTHUR. This is my son Ronald. Ronnie, this is Sir Robert Morton.

RONNIE. How do you do, sir?

ARTHUR. He is going to ask you a few questions. You must answer them all truthfully – as you always have. (*He begins to struggle out of his chair.*) I expect you would like us to leave –

SIR ROBERT. No. Provided, of course, that you don't interrupt. (*To* CATHERINE.) Miss Winslow, will you sit down, please?

CATHERINE *takes a seat abruptly.*

SIR ROBERT. (*To* RONNIE.) Will you stand at the table, facing me? (RONNIE *does so.*) That's right.

SIR ROBERT *and* RONNIE *now face each other across the table.* SIR ROBERT *begins his examination very quietly.*

Now, Ronald, how old are you?

RONNIE. Fourteen and seven months.

SIR ROBERT. You were, then, thirteen and ten months old when you left Osborne: is that right?

RONNIE. Yes, sir.

SIR ROBERT. Now I would like you to cast your mind back to July 7th of last year. Will you tell me in your own words exactly what happened to you on that day?

RONNIE. All right. Well, it was a half-holiday, so we didn't have any work after dinner –

SIR ROBERT. Dinner? At one o clock?

RONNIE. Yes. At least, until prep at seven.

SIR ROBERT. Prep at seven?

RONNIE. Just before dinner I went to the Chief Petty Officer and asked him to let me have fifteen and six out of what I had in the school bank –

SIR ROBERT. Why did you do that?

RONNIE. I wanted to buy an air pistol.

SIR ROBERT. Which cost fifteen and six?

RONNIE. Yes, sir.

SIR ROBERT. And how much money did you have in the school bank at the time?

RONNIE. Two pounds three shillings.

ARTHUR. So you see, sir, what incentive could there possibly be for him to steal five shillings?

SIR ROBERT. (*Coldly.*) I must ask you to be good enough not to interrupt me, sir. (*To* RONNIE.) After you had withdrawn the fifteen and six what did you do?

RONNIE. I had dinner.

SIR ROBERT. Then what?

RONNIE. I went to the locker-room and put the fifteen and six in my locker.

SIR ROBERT. Yes. Then?

RONNIE. I went to get permission to go down to the Post Office. Then I went to the locker-room again, got out my money, and went down to the Post Office.

SIR ROBERT. I see. Go on.

RONNIE. I bought my postal order –

SIR ROBERT. For fifteen and six?

RONNIE. Yes. Then I went back to college. Then I met Elliot minor, and he said: 'I say, isn't it rot? Someone's broken into my locker and pinched a postal order. I've reported it to the P.O.'

SIR ROBERT. Those were Elliot minor's exact words?

RONNIE. He might have used another word for rot –

SIR ROBERT. I see. Continue –

RONNIE. Well, then just before prep I was told to go along and see Commander Flower. The woman from the Post Office was there, and the Commander said. ' Is this the boy? ' and she said: 'It might be. I can't be sure. They all look so much alike.'

ARTHUR. You see? She couldn't identify him.

SIR ROBERT *glares at him.*

SIR ROBERT. (*To* RONNIE.) Go on.

RONNIE. Then she said: ' I only know that the boy who bought a postal order for fifteen and six was the same boy that cashed one for five shillings. ' So the Commander said: 'Did you buy a postal order for fifteen and six?' And I said: 'Yes', and then they made me write Elliot minor's name on an envelope, and compared it to the signature on the postal order – then they sent me to the sanatorium and ten days later I was sacked – I mean – expelled.

SIR ROBERT. I see: (*Quietly.*) Did you cash a postal order belonging to Elliot minor for five shillings?

RONNIE. No, sir.

SIR ROBERT. Did you break into his locker and steal it?

RONNIE. No, sir.

SIR ROBERT. And that is the truth, the whole truth, and nothing but the truth?

RONNIE. Yes, sir.

DICKIE *has come in during this, and is standing furtively in the doorway, not knowing whether to come in or go out.* ARTHUR *waves him impatiently to a seat.*

SIR ROBERT. Right. When the Commander asked you to write Elliot's name on an envelope, how did you write it? With Christian name or initials?

RONNIE. I wrote Charles K. Elliot.

SIR ROBERT. Charles K. Elliot. Did you by any chance happen to see the forged postal order in the Commander's office?

RONNIE. Oh, yes. The Commander showed it to me.

SIR ROBERT. Before or after you had written Elliot's name on the envelope?

RONNIE. After.

SIR ROBERT. After. And did you happen to see how Elliot's name was written on the postal order?

RONNIE. Yes, sir. The same.

SIR ROBERT. The same? Charles K. Elliot?

RONNIE. Yes, sir.

SIR ROBERT. When you wrote on the envelope, what made you choose that particular form?

RONNIE. That was the way he usually signed his name –

SIR ROBERT. How did you know?

RONNIE. Well – he was a great friend of mine –

SIR ROBERT. That is no answer. How did you know?

RONNIE. I'd seen him sign things.

SIR ROBERT. What things?

RONNIE. Oh – ordinary things.

SIR ROBERT. I repeat: what things?

RONNIE. (*Reluctantly.*) Bits of paper.

SIR ROBERT. Bits of paper? And why did he sign his name on bits of paper?

RONNIE. I don't know.

SIR ROBERT. You do know. Why did he sign his name on bits of paper?

RONNIE. He was practising his signature.

SIR ROBERT. And you saw him?

RONNIE. Yes.

SIR ROBERT. Did he know you saw him?

RONNIE. Well – yes –

SIR ROBERT. In other words he showed you exactly how he wrote his signature?

RONNIE. Yes. I suppose he did.

SIR ROBERT. Did you practise writing it yourself?

RONNIE. I might have done.

SIR ROBERT. What do you mean you might have done? Did you or did you not?

RONNIE. Yes –

ARTHUR. (*Sharply.*) Ronnie! You never told me that.

RONNIE. It was only for a joke –

SIR ROBERT. Never mind whether it was for a joke or not. The fact is you practised forging Elliot's signature –

RONNIE. It wasn't forging –

SIR ROBERT. What do you call it then?

RONNIE. Writing.

SIR ROBERT. Very well. Writing. Whoever stole the postal order and cashed it also *wrote* Elliot's signature, didn't he?

RONNIE. Yes.

SIR ROBERT. And, oddly enough, in the exact form in which you had earlier been practising *writing* his signature –

RONNIE. (*Indignantly.*) I say. Which side are you on?

SIR ROBERT. (*Snarling.*) Don't be impertinent! Are you aware that the Admiralty sent up the forged postal order to Mr. Ridgely-Pearce – the greatest handwriting expert in England?

RONNIE. Yes.

SIR ROBERT. And you know that Mr. Ridgeley-Pearce affirmed that there was no doubt that the signature on the postal order and the signature you wrote on the envelope were by one and the same hand?

RONNIE. Yes.

SIR ROBERT. And you still say that you didn't forge that signature?

RONNIE. Yes, I do.

SIR ROBERT. In other words, Mr. Ridgeley-Pearce doesn't know his job?

RONNIE. Well, he's wrong anyway.

SIR ROBERT. When you went into the locker-room after dinner, were you alone?

RONNIE. I don't remember.

SIR ROBERT. I think you do. Were you alone in the locker-room?

RONNIE. Yes.

SIR ROBERT. And you knew which was Elliot's locker?

RONNIE. Yes. Of course.

SIR ROBERT. Why did you go in there at all?

RONNIE. I've told you. To put my fifteen and six away.

SIR ROBERT. Why?

RONNIE. I thought it would be safer.

SIR ROBERT. Why safer than your pocket?

RONNIE. I don't know.

SIR ROBERT. You had it in your pocket at dinner-time. Why this sudden fear for its safety?

RONNIE. (*Plainly rattled.*) I tell you, I don't know –

SIR ROBERT. It was rather an odd thing to do, wasn't it? The money was perfectly safe in your pocket. Why did you suddenly feel yourself impelled to put it away in your locker?

RONNIE. (*Almost shouting.*) I don't know.

SIR ROBERT. Was it because you knew you would be alone in the locker-room at that time?

RONNIE. No.

SIR ROBERT. Where was Elliot's locker in relation to yours?

RONNIE. Next to it, but one.

SIR ROBERT. Next, but one. What time did Elliot put his postal order in his locker?

RONNIE. I don't know. I didn't even know he had a postal order in his locker. I didn't know he had a postal order at all –

SIR ROBERT. Yet you say he was a great friend of yours –

RONNIE. He didn't tell me he had one.

SIR ROBERT. How very secretive of him! What time did you go to the locker-room?

RONNIE. I don't remember.

SIR ROBERT. Was it directly after dinner?

RONNIE. Yes. I think so.

SIR ROBERT. What did you do after leaving the locker-room?

RONNIE. I've told you. I went for permission to go to the Post Office.

SIR ROBERT. What time was that?

RONNIE. About a quarter past two.

SIR ROBERT. Dinner is over at a quarter to two. Which means that you were in the locker-room for half an hour?

RONNIE. I wasn't there all that time –

SIR ROBERT. How long were you there?

RONNIE. About five minutes.

SIR ROBERT. What were you doing for the other twenty-five?

RONNIE. I don't remember.

SIR ROBERT. It's odd that your memory is so good about some things and so bad about others –

RONNIE. Perhaps I waited outside the C.O.'s office.

SIR ROBERT. (*With searing sarcasm.*) Perhaps you waited outside the C.O.'s office! And perhaps no one saw you there either?

RONNIE. No. I don't think they did.

SIR ROBERT. What were you thinking about outside the C.O.'s office for twenty-five minutes?

RONNIE. (*Wildly.*) I don't even know if I was there. I can't remember. Perhaps I wasn't there at all.

SIR ROBERT. No. Perhaps you were still in the locker-room rifling Elliot's locker –

ARTHUR. (*Indignantly.*) Sir Robert, I must ask you –

SIR ROBERT. Quiet!

RONNIE. I remember now. I remember. Someone did see me outside the C.O.'s office. A chap called Casey. I remember I spoke to him.

SIR ROBERT. What did you say?

RONNIE. I said: 'Come down to the Post Office with me. I'm going to cash a postal order.'

SIR ROBERT. (*Triumphantly.*) *Cash* a postal order.

RONNIE. I mean get.

SIR ROBERT. You said cash. Why did you say cash if you meant get.

RONNIE. I don't know.

SIR ROBERT. I suggest cash was the truth.

RONNIE. No, no. It wasn't. It wasn't really. You're muddling me.

SIR ROBERT. You seem easily muddled. How many other lies have you told?

RONNIE. None. Really I haven't –

SIR ROBERT. (*Bending forward malevolently.*) I suggest your whole testimony is a lie –

RONNIE. No! It's the truth –

SIR ROBERT. I suggest there is barely one single word of truth in anything you have said either to me, or to the Judge Advocate, or to the Commander, I suggest that you broke into Elliot's locker, that you stole the postal order for five shillings belonging to Elliot, that you cashed it by means of forging his name –

RONNIE. (*Wailing.*) I didn't. I didn't..

SIR ROBERT. I suggest that you did it for a joke, meaning to give Elliot the five shillings back, but that when you met him and he said he had reported the matter you got frightened and decided to keep quiet –

RONNIE. No, no, no. It isn't true –

SIR ROBERT. I suggest that by continuing to deny your guilt you are causing great hardship to your own family, and considerable annoyance to high and important persons in this country –

CATHERINE. (*On her feet.*) That's a disgraceful thing to say!

ARTHUR. I agree.

SIR ROBERT. (*Leaning forward and glaring at* RONNIE *with the utmost venom.*) I suggest, that the time has at last come for you to undo some of the misery you have caused by confessing to us all now that you are a forger, a liar, and a thief!

RONNIE. (*In tears.*) I'm not! I'm not! I'm not! I didn't do it –

GRACE *has flown to his side and now envelops him.*

ARTHUR. This is outrageous, sir –

JOHN *appears at the door, dressed in evening clothes.*

JOHN. Kate, dear, I'm late. I'm most terribly sorry –

He stops short as he takes in the scene, with RONNIE *sobbing hysterically on his mother's breast, and* ARTHUR *and* CATHERINE *glaring indignantly at* SIR ROBERT, *who is engaged in putting his papers together.*

SIR ROBERT. (*To* DESMOND.) Can I drop you anywhere? My car is at the door.

DESMOND. Er – no – I thank you –

SIR ROBERT. (*Carelessly.*) Well, send all this stuff round to my chambers tomorrow morning, will you?

DESMOND. But – but will you need it now?

SIR ROBERT. Oh, yes. The boy is plainly innocent. I accept the brief.

He bows to ARTHUR *and* CATHERINE *and walks languidly to the door, past the bewildered* JOHN, *to whom he gives a polite nod as he goes out.* RONNIE *continues to sob hysterically.*

Curtain.

Act Three

*Scene: the same, nine months later. The time is about ten-thirty
p.m.* ARTHUR *is sitting in his favourite armchair, reading aloud
from an evening paper, whose wide headline:* 'WINSLOW DEBATE:
FIRST LORD REPLIES' *we can read on the front page. Listening to him
are* RONNIE *and* GRACE, *though neither of them seems to be
doing so with much concentration.* RONNIE *is finding it hard to
keep his eyes open, and* GRACE, *darning socks in the other
armchair, has evidently other and, to her, more important matters
on her mind.*

ARTHUR. *(Reading.)* – 'The Admiralty, during the whole of this
long-drawn-out dispute, have at no time acted hastily or
ill-advisedly, and it is a matter of mere histrionic hyperbole for
the right honourable and learned gentleman opposite to
characterize the conduct of my department as that of
callousness so inhuman as to amount to deliberate malice
towards the boy Winslow. Such unfounded accusations I can
well choose to ignore. (An honourable Member: "You can't.")
Honourable Members opposite may interrupt as much as they
please, but I repeat – there is nothing whatever that the
Admiralty has done, or failed to do, in the case of this cadet for
which I, as First Lord, need to apologize. (Further Opposition
interruptions.)' *(He stops reading and looks up.)* I must say it
looks as if the First Lord's having rather a rough passage – *(He
breaks off, noticing* RONNIE'S *head has fallen back on the
cushions and he is asleep.)* I trust my reading isn't keeping you
awake. *(There is no answer.)* I say I trust my reading isn't
keeping you awake! *(Again there is no answer. Helplessly.)*
Grace!

GRACE. My poor sleepy little lamb! It's long past his bedtime,
Arthur.

ARTHUR. Grace, dear – at this very moment your poor sleepy
little lamb is the subject of a very violent and heated debate in
the House of Commons. I should have thought, in the
circumstances, it might have been possible for him to contrive
to stay awake for a few minutes past his bedtime –

GRACE. I expect he's over-excited.

ARTHUR *and* GRACE *both look at the tranquilly oblivious
form on the sofa.*

ARTHUR. A picture of over-excitement. (*Sharply.*) Ronnie! (*No answer.*) Ronnie!

RONNIE. (*Opening his eyes.*) Yes, Father?

ARTHUR. I am reading the account of the debate. Would you like to listen, or would you rather go to bed?

RONNIE. Oh, I'd like to listen, of course, Father. I was listening, too, only I had my eyes shut –

ARTHUR. Very well. (*Reading.*) ' The First Lord continued amid further interruptions: The chief point of criticism against the Admiralty appears to centre in the purely legal question of the Petition of Right brought by Mr. Arthur Winslow and the Admiralty's demurrer thereto. Sir Robert Morton has made great play with his eloquent reference to the liberty of the individual menaced, as he puts it, by the new despotism of bureaucracy – and I was as moved as any honourable Member opposite by his resonant use of the words: Let Right be done – the time-honoured phrase with which in his opinion the Attorney-General should without question have endorsed Mr. Winslow's Petition of Right. Nevertheless, the matter is not nearly as simple as he appears to imagine. Cadet Ronald Winslow is a servant of the Crown, and has therefore no more right than any other member of His Majesty's forces to sue the Crown in open court. To allow him to do so would undoubtedly raise the most dangerous precedents. There is no doubt whatever in my mind that in certain cases private rights may have to be sacrificed for the public good –' (He *looks up*.) And what other excuse, pray, did Charles the First make for ship money and –

RONNIE, *after a manful attempt to keep his eyes open by self-pinchings and other devices, has once more succumbed to oblivion.*

(*Sharply.*) Ronnie! Ronnie!

RONNIE *stirs, turns over, and slides more comfortably into the cushions.*

Would you believe it!

GRACE. He's dead tired. I'd better take him up to his bed –

ARTHUR. No. If he must sleep, let him sleep there.

GRACE. Oh, but he'd be much more comfy in his little bed –

ARTHUR. I dare say: but the debate continues and until it's ended the cause of it all will certainly not make himself comfy in his little bed.

VIOLET *comes in.*

VIOLET. There are three more reporters in the hall, sir. Want to see you very urgently. Shall I let them in?

ARTHUR. No. Certainly not. I issued a statement yesterday. Until the debate is over I have nothing more to say.

VIOLET. Yes, sir. That's what I told them, but they wouldn't go.

ARTHUR. Well, make them. Use force, if necessary.

VIOLET. Yes, sir. And shall I cut some sandwiches for Miss Catherine, as she missed her dinner?

GRACE. Yes, Violet. Good idea.

VIOLET *goes out.*

VIOLET. (*Off.*) It's no good. No more statements.

Voices answer her, fading at length into silence. GRACE *puts a rug over* RONNIE, *now sleeping very soundly.*

ARTHUR. Grace, dear –

GRACE. Yes?

ARTHUR. I fancy this might be a good opportunity of talking to Violet.

GRACE. (*Quite firmly.*) No, dear.

ARTHUR. Meaning that it isn't a good opportunity? Or meaning that you have no intention at all of ever talking to Violet?

GRACE. I'll do it one day, Arthur. Tomorrow, perhaps. Not now.

ARTHUR. I believe you'd do better to grasp the nettle. Delay only adds to your worries –

GRACE. (*Bitterly.*) My worries? What do you know about my worries?

ARTHUR. A good deal, Grace. But I feel they would be a lot lessened if you faced the situation squarely.

GRACE. It's easy for you to talk, Arthur. You don't have to do it.

ARTHUR. I will, if you like.

GRACE. No, dear.

ARTHUR. If you explain the dilemma to her carefully – if you even show her the figures I jotted down for you yesterday – I venture to think you won't find her unreasonable.

GRACE. It won't be easy for her to find another place.

ARTHUR We'll give her an excellent reference.

GRACE. That won't alter the fact that she's never been properly trained as a parlourmaid and – well – you know yourself how we're always having to explain her to people. No, Arthur, I don't mind how many figures she's shown, it's a brutal thing to do.

ARTHUR. Facts are brutal things.

GRACE. (*A shade hysterically.*) Facts? I don't think I know what facts are any more –

ARTHUR. The facts, at this moment, are that we have a half of the income we had a year ago and we're living at nearly the same rate. However you look at it that's bad economics –

GRACE. I'm not talking about economics, Arthur. I'm talking about ordinary, common or garden facts – things we took for granted a year ago and which now don't seem to matter any more.

ARTHUR. Such as?

GRACE. (*With rising voice.*) Such as a happy home and peace and quiet and an ordinary respectable life, and some sort of future for us and our children. In the last year you've thrown all that overboard, Arthur. There's your return for it, I suppose. (*She indicates the headline in the paper.*) And it's all very exciting and important, I'm sure, but it doesn't bring back any of the things that we've lost. I can only pray to God that you know what you're doing.

RONNIE *stirs in his sleep.* GRACE *lowers her voice at the end of her speech. There is a pause.*

ARTHUR. I know exactly what I'm doing, Grace. I'm going to publish my son's innocence before the world, and for that end I am not prepared to weigh the cost.

GRACE. But the cost may be out of all proportion –

ARTHUR. It may be. That doesn't concern me. I hate heroics, Grace, but you force me to say this. An injustice has been done. I am going to set it right, and there is no sacrifice in the world I am not prepared to make in order to do so.

GRACE. (*With sudden violence.*) Oh, I wish I could see the sense of it all! (*Pointing to* RONNIE.) He's perfectly happy, at a good school, doing very well. No one need ever have known about Osborne, if you hadn't gone and shouted it out to the whole world. As it is, whatever happens now, he'll go through the rest of his life as the boy in that Winslow case – the boy who stole that postal order –

ARTHUR. (*Grimly.*) The boy who didn't steal that postal order.

GRACE. (*Wearily.*) What's the difference? When millions are talking and gossiping about him, a did or a didn't hardly matters. The Winslow boy is enough. You talk about sacrificing everything for him: but when he's grown up he won't thank you for it, Arthur – even though you've given your life to – publish his innocence as you call it.

ARTHUR *makes an impatient gesture.*

Yes, Arthur – your life. You talk gaily about arthritis and a touch of gout and old age and the rest of it, but you know as well as any of the doctors what really is the matter with you. (*Nearly in tears.*) You're destroying yourself, Arthur, and me and your family besides. For what, I'd like to know? I've asked you and Kate to tell me a hundred times but you never will. For what, Arthur?

ARTHUR *has struggled painfully out of his seat and now approaches her.*

ARTHUR. (*Quietly.*) For Justice, Grace.

GRACE. That sounds very noble. Are you sure it's true? Are you sure it isn't just plain pride and self-importance and sheer brute stubbornness?

ARTHUR. (*Putting a hand out.*) No, Grace. I don't think it is. I really don't think it is –

GRACE. (*Shaking off his hand.*) No. This time I'm not going to cry and say I'm sorry, and make it all up again. I can stand anything if there is a reason for it. But for no reason at all, it's unfair to ask so much of me. It's unfair –

She breaks down. As ARTHUR *puts a comforting arm around her she pushes him off and goes out of the door.* RONNIE *has, meanwhile, opened his eyes.*

RONNIE. What's the matter, Father?

ARTHUR. (*Turning from the door.*) Your mother is a little upset –

RONNIE. (*Drowsily.*) Why? Aren't things going well?

ARTHUR. Oh, yes. (*Murmuring.*) Very well. (*He sits with more than his usual difficulty, as if he were utterly exhausted.*) Very well indeed.

RONNIE *contentedly closes his eyes again.*

(*Gently.*) You'd better go to bed now, Ronnie. You'll be more comfortable –

He sees RONNIE *is asleep again. He makes as if to wake him, then shrugs his shoulders and turns away.* VIOLET *comes in with sandwiches on a plate and a letter on a salver.*

Thank you, Violet.

VIOLET *puts the sandwiches on the table and hands* ARTHUR *the letter.* ARTHUR *puts it down on the table beside him without opening it.* VIOLET *turns to go out.*

ARTHUR. Oh, Violet –

VIOLET. (*Turning placidly.*) Yes, sir?

ARTHUR. How long have you been with us?

VIOLET. Twenty-four years come April, sir.

ARTHUR. As long as that?

VIOLET. Yes, sir. Miss Kate was that high when I first came. (*She indicates a small child.*) and Mr. Dickie hadn't even been thought of –

ARTHUR. I remember you coming to us now. I remember it well. What do you think of this case, Violet?

VIOLET. A fine old rumpus that is, and no mistake.

ARTHUR. It is, isn't it? A fine old rumpus.

VIOLET. There was a bit in the *Evening News*. Did you read it, sir.

ARTHUR. No. What did it say?

VIOLET. Oh, about how it was a fuss about nothing and a shocking waste of the Government's time, but how it was a good thing all the same because it could only happen in England –

ARTHUR. There seems to be a certain lack of logic in that argument –

VIOLET. Well, perhaps they put it a bit different, sir. Still, that's what it said all right. And when you think it's all because of our Master Ronnie – I have to laugh about it sometimes. I really do. Wasting the Government's time at his age! I never did. Well, wonders will never cease.

ARTHUR. I know. Wonders will never cease.

VIOLET. Well – would that be all, sir?

ARTHUR. Yes, Violet. That'll be all.

CATHERINE *comes in.*

CATHERINE. Good evening, Violet.

VIOLET. Good evening, miss.

She goes out.

CATHERINE. Hullo, Father. (*She kisses him. Indicating* RONNIE.) An honourable Member described that this evening as a piteous

little figure, crying aloud to humanity for justice and redress.
I wish he could see him now.

ARTHUR. (*Testily*.) It's long past his bedtime. What's happened? Is
the debate over?

CATHERINE. As good as. The First Lord gave an assurance that in
future there would be no inquiry at Osborne or Dartmouth
without informing the parents first. That seemed to satisfy
most Members –

ARTHUR. But what about *our* case? Is he going to allow us a fair
trial?

CATHERINE. Apparently not.

ARTHUR. But that's iniquitous. I thought he would be forced to –

CATHERINE. I thought so, too. The House evidently thought
otherwise.

ARTHUR. Will there be a division?

CATHERINE. There may be. If there is the Government will win.

ARTHUR. What is the motion?

CATHERINE. To reduce the First Lord's salary by a hundred
pounds. (*With a faint smile*.) Naturally no one really wants to do
that. (*Indicating sandwiches*.) Are these for me?

ARTHUR. Yes.

CATHERINE *starts to eat the sandwiches*.

So we're back where we started, then?

CATHERINE. It looks like it.

ARTHUR. The debate has done us no good at all?

CATHERINE. It's aired the case a little, perhaps. A few more
thousand people will say to each other at breakfast tomorrow:
'That boy ought to be allowed a fair trial.'

ARTHUR. What's the good of that, if they can't make themselves
heard?

CATHERINE. I think they can – given time.

ARTHUR. Given time?

Pause.

But didn't Sir Robert make any protest when the First Lord
refused a trial?

CATHERINE. Not a verbal protest. Something far more
spectacular and dramatic. He'd had his feet on the Treasury
table and his hat over his eyes during most of the First Lord's

speech – and he suddenly got up very deliberately, glared at the First Lord, threw a whole bundle of notes on the floor, and stalked out of the House. It made a magnificent effect. If I hadn't known I could have sworn he was genuinely indignant –

ARTHUR. Of course he was genuinely indignant. So would any man of feeling be –

CATHERINE. Sir Robert, Father dear, is not a man of feeling. I don't think any emotion at all can stir that fishy heart –

ARTHUR. Except perhaps a single-minded love of justice.

CATHERINE. Nonsense. A single-minded love of Sir Robert Morton.

ARTHUR. You're very ungrateful to him considering all he's done for us these last months –

CATHERINE. I'm not ungrateful, Father. He's been wonderful – I admit it freely. No one could have fought a harder fight.

ARTHUR. Well, then –

CATHERINE. It's only his motives I question. At least I *don't* question them at all. I know them.

ARTHUR. What are they?

CATHERINE. First – publicity – you know – look at me, the staunch defender of the little man – and then second – a nice popular stick to beat the Government with. Both very useful to an ambitious man. Luckily for him we've provided them.

ARTHUR. Luckily for us too, Kate.

CATHERINE. Oh, I agree. But don't fool yourself about him, Father, for all that. The man is a fish, a hard, cold-blooded, supercilious, sneering fish.

VIOLET *enters*.

VIOLET. (*Announcing*.) Sir Robert Morton.

CATHERINE *chokes over her sandwich*. SIR ROBERT *comes in*.

SIR ROBERT. Good evening.

CATHERINE. (*Still choking*.) Good evening.

SIR ROBERT. Something gone down the wrong way?

CATHERINE. Yes.

SIR ROBERT. May I assist? (*He pats her on the back*.)

CATHERINE. Thank you.

SIR ROBERT. (*To* ARTHUR.) Good evening sir. I thought I would call and give you an account of the day's proceedings, but I see your daughter has forestalled me.

CATHERINE. Did you know I was in the gallery?

SIR ROBERT. (*Gallantly.*) With such a charming hat, how could I have missed you?

ARTHUR. It was very good of you to call, sir, nevertheless –

SIR ROBERT. (*Seeing* RONNIE.) Ah. The *casus belli* – dormant –

ARTHUR *goes to wake him.*

SIR ROBERT. No, no. I beg of you. Please do not disturb his innocent slumbers.

CATHERINE. *Innocent* slumbers?

SIR ROBERT. Exactly. Besides, I fear since our first encounter he is, rather pardonably, a trifle nervous of me.

CATHERINE. Will you betray a technical secret, Sir Robert? What happened in that first examination to make you so sure of his innocence?

SIR ROBERT. Three things. First of all, he made far too many damaging admissions. A guilty person would have been much more careful and on his guard. Secondly, I laid him a trap; and thirdly, left him a loophole. Anyone who was guilty would have fallen into the one and darted through the other. He did neither.

CATHERINE. The trap was to ask him suddenly what time Elliot put the postal order in his locker, wasn't it?

SIR ROBERT. Yes.

ARTHUR. And the loophole?

SIR ROBERT. I then suggested to him that he had stolen the postal order for a joke – which, had he been guilty, he would surely have admitted to as being the lesser of two evils.

CATHERINE. I see. It was very cleverly thought out.

SIR ROBERT. (*With a little bow.*) Thank you.

ARTHUR. May we offer you some refreshment, Sir Robert? A whisky and soda?

SIR ROBERT. No thank you. Nothing at all.

ARTHUR. My daughter has told me of your demonstration during the First Lord's speech. She described it as – magnificent.

SIR ROBERT. (*With a glance at* CATHERINE.) Did she? That was good of her. It's a very old trick, you know. I've done it many times in the Courts. It's nearly always surprisingly effective –

CATHERINE *catches her father's eye and nods triumphantly.*

(*To* CATHERINE.) Was the First Lord at all put out by it – did you notice?

CATHERINE. How could he have failed to be? (*To* ARTHUR, *approaching his chair.*) I wish you could have seen it, Father – it was – (*She notices the letter on the table beside* ARTHUR *and snatches it up with a sudden gesture. She examines the envelope.*) When did this come?

ARTHUR. A few minutes ago. Do you know the writing?

CATHERINE. Yes. (*She puts the letter back on the table.*)

ARTHUR. Whose is it?

CATHERINE. I shouldn't bother to read it, if I were you. ARTHUR *looks at her, puzzled, then takes up the letter.*

ARTHUR. (*To* SIR ROBERT.) Will you forgive me?

SIR ROBERT. Of course.

ARTHUR *opens the letter and begins to read.* CATHERINE *watches him for a moment, and then turns with a certain forced liveliness to* SIR ROBERT.

CATHERINE. Well, what do you think the next step should be?

SIR ROBERT. I have already been considering that, Miss Winslow. I believe that perhaps the best plan would be to renew our efforts to get the Director of Public Prosecutions to act.

CATHERINE. (*With one eye on her father.*) But do you think there's any chance of that?

SIR ROBERT. Oh, yes. In the main it will chiefly be a question of making ourselves a confounded nuisance –

CATHERINE. We've certainly done that quite successfully so far – thanks to you –

SIR ROBERT. (*Suavely.*) Ah. That is perhaps the only quality I was born with – the ability to make myself a confounded nuisance.

He, too, has his eye on ARTHUR, *sensing something amiss.* ARTHUR *finishes reading the letter.*

CATHERINE. (*With false vivacity.*) Father – Sir Robert thinks we might get the Director of Public Prosecutions to act –

ARTHUR. What?

SIR ROBERT. We were discussing how to proceed with the case –

ARTHUR. The case? (*He stares, a little blankly, from one to the other.*) Yes. We must think of that, mustn't we? (*Pause.*) How to proceed with the case? (*To* SIR ROBERT, *abruptly.*) I'm afraid I don't think, all things considered, that much purpose would be served by going on –

SIR ROBERT *and* CATHERINE *stare at him blankly.*

CATHERINE *goes quickly to him and snatches the letter from his lap. She begins to read.*

SIR ROBERT. (*With a sudden change of tone.*) Of course we must go on.

ARTHUR. (*In a low voice.*) It is not for you to choose, sir. The choice is mine.

SIR ROBERT. (*Harshly.*) Then you must reconsider it. To give up now would be insane.

ARTHUR. Insane? My sanity has already been called in question tonight – for carrying the case as far as I have.

SIR ROBERT. Whatever the contents of that letter, or whatever has happened to make you lose heart, I insist that we continue the fight –

ARTHUR. Insist? We? It is my fight – my fight alone – and it is for me alone to judge when the time has come to give up.

SIR ROBERT. (*Violently.*) But why give up? Why? In heaven's name, man, why?

ARTHUR. (*Slowly.*) I have made many sacrifices for this case. Some of them I had no right to make, but I made them none the less. But there is a limit and I have reached it. I am sorry, Sir Robert. More sorry, perhaps, than you are, but the Winslow case is now closed.

SIR ROBERT. Balderdash!

ARTHUR *looks surprised at this unparliamentary expression.* CATHERINE *has read and re-read the letter, and now breaks the silence in a calm, methodical voice.*

CATHERINE. My father doesn't mean what he says, Sir Robert.

SIR ROBERT. I am glad to hear it.

CATHERINE. Perhaps I should explain this letter –

ARTHUR. No, Kate.

CATHERINE. Sir Robert knows so much about our family affairs, Father, I don't see it will matter much if he learns a little more. (*To* SIR ROBERT.) This letter is from a certain Colonel Watherstone who is the father of the man I'm engaged to. We've always known he was opposed to the case, so it really comes as no surprise. In it he says that our efforts to discredit the Admiralty in the House of Commons today have resulted merely in our making the name of Winslow a nation-wide laughing-stock. I think that's his phrase. (*She consults the letter.*) Yes. That's right. A nation-wide laughing-stock.

SIR ROBERT. I don't care for his English.

CATHERINE. It's not very good, is it? He goes on to say that unless my father will give him a firm undertaking to drop this whining and reckless agitation – I suppose he means the case – he will exert every bit of influence he has over his son to prevent him marrying me.

SIR ROBERT. I see. An ultimatum.

CATHERINE. Yes – but a pointless one.

SIR ROBERT. He has no influence over his son?

CATHERINE. Oh, yes. A little, naturally. But his son is of age, and his own master –

SIR ROBERT. Is he dependent on his father for money?

CATHERINE. He gets an allowance. But he can live perfectly well – we both can live perfectly well without it.

Pause. SIR ROBERT *stares hard at her, then turns abruptly to* ARTHUR.

SIR ROBERT. Well, sir?

ARTHUR. I'm afraid I can't go back on what I have already said. I will give you a decision in a few days –

SIR ROBERT. Your daughter seems prepared to take the risk –

ARTHUR. I am not. Not, at least, until I know how great a risk it is –

SIR ROBERT. How do you estimate the risk, Miss Winslow?

Pause. CATHERINE, *for all her bravado, is plainly scared. She is engaged in lighting a cigarette as* SIR ROBERT *asks his question.*

CATHERINE. (*At length.*) Negligible.

SIR ROBERT *stares at her again. Feeling his eyes on her, she returns his glance defiantly. Pause.*

SIR ROBERT. (*Returning abruptly to his languid manner.*) I see. May I take a cigarette, too?

CATHERINE. Yes, of course. I thought you didn't smoke.

SIR ROBERT. Only occasionally. (*To* ARTHUR.) I really must apologize to you, sir, for speaking to you as I did just now. It was unforgivable.

ARTHUR. Not at all, sir. You were upset at giving up the case – and, to be frank, I liked you for it –

SIR ROBERT. (*With a deprecating gesture.*) It has been rather a tiring day. The House of Commons is a peculiarly exhausting place, you know. Too little ventilation, and far too much hot air – I really am most truly sorry.

ARTHUR. Please.

SIR ROBERT. (*Carelessly.*) Of course, you must decide about the case as you wish. That really is a most charming hat, Miss Winslow –

CATHERINE. I'm glad you like it.

SIR ROBERT. It seems decidedly wrong to me that a lady of your political persuasion should be allowed to adorn herself with such a very feminine allurement. It really looks so awfully like trying to have the best of both worlds –

CATHERINE. I'm not a militant, you know, Sir Robert. I don't go about breaking shop windows with a hammer or pouring acid down pillar boxes.

SIR ROBERT. (*Languidly.*) I am truly glad to hear it. Both those activities would be highly unsuitable in that hat –

CATHERINE *glares at him but suppresses an angry retort.*

I have never yet fully grasped what active steps you take to propagate your cause, Miss Winslow.

CATHERINE. (*Shortly.*) I'm an organizing secretary at the West London Branch of the Woman's Suffrage Association.

SIR ROBERT. Indeed? Is the work hard?

CATHERINE. Very.

SIR ROBERT. But not, I should imagine, particularly lucrative.

CATHERINE. The work is voluntary and unpaid.

SIR ROBERT. (*Murmuring.*) Dear me! What sacrifices you young ladies seem prepared to make for your convictions –

VIOLET *enters.*

VIOLET. (*To* CATHERINE.) Mr. Watherstone is in the hall, miss. Says he would like to have a word with you in private – most particular –

Pause.

CATHERINE. Oh. I'll come out to him –

ARTHUR. No. See him in here.

He begins to struggle out of his chair. SIR ROBERT *assists him.*

You wouldn't mind coming to the dining-room, would you, Sir Robert, for a moment?

SIR ROBERT. Not in the least.

CATHERINE. All right, Violet.

VIOLET. Will you come in, sir.

JOHN *comes in. He is looking depressed and anxious.* CATHERINE *greets him with a smile, which he returns only half-heartedly. This exchange is lost on* ARTHUR, *who has his back to them, but not on* SIR ROBERT.

CATHERINE. Hello, John.

JOHN. Hullo. (*To* ARTHUR.) Good evening, sir.

ARTHUR. Good evening, John. (*He goes on towards dining-room.*)

CATHERINE. I don't think you've met Sir Robert Morton.

JOHN. No, I haven't. How do you do, sir?

SIR ROBERT. I think you promised me a whisky and soda. (*Turning to* JOHN.) May I offer my very belated congratulations?

JOHN. Congratulations? Oh, yes. Thank you.

ARTHUR *and* SIR ROBERT *go into dining-room. There is a pause.* CATHERINE *is watching* JOHN *with an anxious expression.*

JOHN. (*Indicating* RONNIE.) Is he asleep?

CATHERINE. Yes.

JOHN. Sure he's not shamming?

CATHERINE. Yes.

JOHN. (*After a pause.*) My father's written your father a letter.

CATHERINE. I know. I've read it.

JOHN. Oh.

CATHERINE. Did you?

JOHN. Yes. He showed it to me.

Pause. JOHN *is carefully not looking at her.*

(*At length.*) Well, what's his answer?

CATHERINE. My father? I don't suppose he'll send one.

JOHN. You think he'll ignore it?

CATHERINE. Isn't that the best answer to blackmail?

JOHN. (*Muttering.*) It was damned high-handed of the old man, I admit.

CATHERINE. High-handed?

JOHN. I tried to get him not to send it –

CATHERINE. I'm glad.

JOHN. The trouble is – he's perfectly serious.

CATHERINE. I never thought he wasn't.

JOHN. If your father does decide to go on with the case, I'm very much afraid he'll do everything he threatens.

CATHERINE. Forbid the match?

JOHN. Yes.

CATHERINE. (*Almost pleadingly.*) Isn't that rather an empty threat, John?

JOHN. (*Slowly.*) Well, there's always the allowance –

CATHERINE. (*Dully.*) Yes, I see. There's always the allowance.

JOHN. I tell you, Kate darling, this is going to need damned careful handling; otherwise we'll find ourselves in the soup.

CATHERINE. Without your allowance would we be in the soup?

JOHN. And without your settlement. My dear girl, of course we would. Dash it all, I can't even live on my pay as it is, but with two of us –

CATHERINE. I've heard it said that two can live as cheaply as one.

JOHN. Don't you believe it. Two can live as cheaply as two, and that's all there is to it.

CATHERINE. Yes, I see. I didn't know.

JOHN. Unlike you I have a practical mind, Kate. I'm sorry, but it's no good dashing blindly ahead without thinking of these things first. The problem has got to be faced.

CATHERINE. I'm ready to face it, John. What do you suggest?

JOHN. (*Cautiously.*) Well – I think you should consider very carefully before you take the next step –

CATHERINE. I can assure you we will, John. The question is – what *is* the next step?

JOHN. Well – this is the way I see it. I'm going to be honest now. I hope you don't mind –

CATHERINE. No. I should welcome it.

JOHN. Your young brother over there pinches or doesn't pinch a five-bob postal order. For over a year you and your father fight a magnificent fight on his behalf, and I'm sure everyone admires you for it –

CATHERINE. Your father hardly seems to –

JOHN. Well, he's a diehard. Like these old Admirals you've been up against. I meant ordinary reasonable people, like myself. But now look – you've had two inquiries, the Petition of Right case which the Admiralty had thrown out of Court, and the Appeal. And now, good heavens, you've had the whole damned House of Commons getting themselves worked up into a frenzy about it. Surely, darling, that's enough for you? My God! Surely the case can end there?

CATHERINE. (*Slowly.*) Yes. I suppose the case can end there.

JOHN. (*Pointing to* RONNIE.) *He* won't mind.

CATHERINE. No. I know he won't.

JOHN. Look at him! Perfectly happy and content. Not a care in the world. How do you know what's going on in his mind? How can you be so sure he didn't do it?

CATHERINE. (*Also gazing down at* RONNIE.) I'm not so sure he didn't do it.

JOHN. (*Appalled.*) Good Lord! Then why in heaven's name have you and your father spent all this time and money trying to prove his innocence?

CATHERINE. (*Quietly.*) His innocence or guilt aren't important to me. They are to my father. Not to me. I believe he didn't do it; but I may be wrong. To prove that he didn't do it is of hardly more interest to me than the identity of the college servant, or whoever it was, who did it. All that I care about is that people should know that a Government Department has ignored a fundamental human right and that it should be forced to acknowledge it. That's all that's important to me.

JOHN. But, darling, after all those long noble words, it does really resolve itself to a question of a fourteen-year-old kid and a five-bob postal order, doesn't it?

CATHERINE. Yes, it does.

JOHN. (*Reasonably.*) Well now, look. There's a European war blowing up, there's a coal strike on, there's a fair chance of civil war in Ireland, and there's a hundred and one other things on the horizon at the moment that I think you genuinely could call *important*. And yet, with all that on its mind, the House of Commons takes a whole day to discuss him (*Pointing to* RONNIE.) and his bally postal order. Surely you must see that's a little out of proportion –

Pause. CATHERINE *raises her head slowly.*

CATHERINE. (*With some spirit.*) All I know is, John, that if ever the time comes that the House of Commons has so much on its mind that it can't find time to discuss a Ronnie Winslow and his bally postal order, this country will be a far poorer place than it is now. (*Wearily.*) But you needn't go on, John dear. You've said quite enough. I entirely see your point of view.

JOHN. I don't know whether you realize that all this publicity you're getting is making the name of Winslow a bit of a – well –

CATHERINE. (*Steadily.*) A nation-wide laughing-stock, your father said.

JOHN. Well, that's putting it a bit steep. But people do find the case a bit ridiculous, you know. I mean, I get chaps coming up to me in the mess all the time and saying: 'I say, is it true you're going to marry the Winslow girl? You'd better be careful. You'll find yourself up in front of the House of Lords for pinching the Adjutant's bath.' Things like that. They're not awfully funny –

CATHERINE. That's nothing. They're singing a verse about us at the Alhambra –

Winslow one day went to heaven
And found a poor fellow in quod.
The fellow said I didn't do it,
So naturally Winslow sued God.

JOHN. Well, darling – you see –

CATHERINE. Yes. I see. (*Quietly.*) Do you want to marry me, John?

JOHN. What?

CATHERINE. I said: Do you want to marry me?

JOHN. Well, of course I do. You know I do. We've been engaged for over a year now. Have I ever wavered before?

CATHERINE. No. Never before.

JOHN. (*Correcting himself.*) I'm not wavering now. Not a bit – I'm only telling you what I think is the best course for us to take.

CATHERINE. But isn't it already too late? Even if we gave up the case, would you still want to marry – the Winslow girl?

JOHN. All that would blow over in no time.

CATHERINE. (*Slowly.*) And we'd have the allowance –

JOHN. Yes. We would.

CATHERINE. And that's so important –

JOHN. (*Quietly.*) It is, darling. I'm sorry, but you can't shame me into saying it isn't.

CATHERINE. I didn't mean to shame you –

JOHN. Oh, yes you did. I know that tone of voice.

CATHERINE. (*Humbly.*) I'm sorry.

JOHN. (*Confidently.*) Well, now – what's the answer?

CATHERINE. (*Slowly.*) I love you, John, and I want to be your wife.

JOHN. Well, then, that's all I want to know. Darling! I was sure nothing so stupid and trivial could possibly come between us.

He kisses her. She responds wearily. The telephone rings. After a pause she releases herself and picks up the receiver.

CATHERINE. Hullo . . . Yes . . . Will you wait a minute? (*She goes to the dining-room door and calls.*) Sir Robert! Someone wants you on the telephone –

SIR ROBERT *comes out of the dining room.*

SIR ROBERT. Thank you. I'm so sorry to interrupt.

CATHERINE. You didn't. We'd finished our talk.

SIR ROBERT *looks at her inquiringly. She gives him no sign. He walks to the telephone.*

SIR ROBERT. (*Noticing sandwiches.*) How delicious. May I help myself?

CATHERINE. Do.

SIR ROBERT. (*Into receiver.*) Hello . . . Yes, Michael . . . F.E.? I didn't know he was going to speak . . . I see . . . Go on . . .

SIR ROBERT *listens, with closed eyelids, munching a sandwich, meanwhile.*

(*At length.*) Thank you, Michael.

He rings off. ARTHUR *has appeared in the dining-room doorway.*

SIR ROBERT. (*To* ARTHUR.) There has been a most interesting development in the House, sir.

ARTHUR. What?

SIR ROBERT. My secretary tells me that a barrister friend of mine who, quite unknown to me, was interested in the case, got on his feet shortly after nine-thirty and delivered one of the most scathing denunciations of a Government Department ever heard in the House. (*To* CATHERINE.) What a shame we missed it – his style is quite superb –

ARTHUR. What happened?

SIR ROBERT. The debate revived, of course, and the First Lord, who must have felt himself fairly safe, suddenly found himself under attack from all parts of the House. It appears that rather than risk a division he has this moment given an undertaking that he will instruct the Attorney-General to endorse our Petition of Right. The case of Winslow versus Rex can now therefore come to Court.

There is a pause. ARTHUR *and* CATHERINE *stare at him unbelievingly.*

(*At length.*) Well, sir. What are my instructions?

ARTHUR. (*Slowly.*) The decision is no longer mine, sir. You must ask my daughter.

SIR ROBERT. What are my instructions, Miss Winslow?

CATHERINE *looks down at the sleeping* RONNIE. ARTHUR *is watching her intently.* SIR ROBERT, *munching sandwiches, is also looking at her.*

CATHERINE. (*In a flat voice.*) Do you need my instructions, Sir Robert? Aren't they already on the Petition? Doesn't it say: Let Right be done?

JOHN *makes a move of protest towards her. She does not look at him. He turns abruptly to the door.*

JOHN. (*Furiously.*) Kate! Good night.

He goes out. SIR ROBERT, *with languid speculation, watches him go.*

SIR ROBERT. (*His mouth full.*) Well, then – we must endeavour to see that it is.

Curtain.

Act Four

Scene: the same, about five months later. It is a stiflingly hot June day – nearly two years less one month since RONNIE'S *dismissal from Osborne. The glass door to the garden stands open, and a bath chair, unoccupied, has been placed near by. On the rise of the curtain the stage is empty and the telephone is ringing insistently.*

DICKIE *comes in from the hall carrying a suitcase, evidently very hot, his straw hat pushed on to the back of his head and panting from his exertions. He is wearing a neat, dark blue suit, a sober tie, and a stiff collar. He puts the suitcase down and mops his face with his handkerchief. Then he goes to the hall door and calls:*

DICKIE. Mother! (*There is no reply.*) Violet! (*Again no reply.*) Anyone about?

He goes to the telephone – taking off the receiver.

Hullo . . . No, not senior – junior . . . I don't know where he is . . . *Daily Mail?* . . . No, I'm the brother . . . Elder brother – that's right . . . Well – I'm in the banking business . . . That's right. Following in father's footsteps . . . My views on the case? Well – I – er – I don't know I have any, except, I mean, I hope we win and all that . . . No, I haven't been in Court. I've only just arrived from Reading . . . Reading . . . Yes. That's where I work . . . Yes, I've come up for the last two days of the trial. Verdict's expected tomorrow, isn't it? . . . Twenty-two, last March . . . *Seven* years older . . . No. He was thirteen when it happened, but now he's fifteen . . . Well, I suppose, if I'm anything I'm a sort of Liberal-Conservative . . . Single . . . No. No immediate prospects. I say, is this at all interesting to you? . . . Well, a perfectly ordinary kid, just like any other – makes a noise, does fretwork, doesn't wash and all that . . . Doesn't wash . . . (*Alarmed.*) I say, don't take that too literally. I mean he does, sometimes . . . Yes. All right. Goodbye . . .

He rings off and exits through centre door. Telephone rings again. He comes back to answer it, when GRACE *dressed for going out, comes out of the dining-room.*

GRACE. Oh, hullo, darling. When did you get here?

She picks up the telephone receiver.

(*Into receiver.*) Everyone out.

She rings off and embraces DICKIE.

You're thinner. I like your new suit.

DICKIE. Straight from Reading's Savile Row. Off the peg at three and a half guineas. (*Pointing to telephone.*) I say – does that go on all the time?

GRACE. All blessed day. The last four days it simply hasn't stopped.

DICKIE. I had to fight my way in through an army of reporters and people –

GRACE. Yes, I know. You didn't say anything, I hope, Dickie dear. It's better not to say a word –

DICKIE. I don't think I said anything much . . . (*Carelessly.*) Oh, yes. I did say that I personally thought he did it –

GRACE. (*Horrified.*) Dickie! You didn't! (*He is smiling at her.*) Oh, I see. It's a joke. You mustn't say things like that, even in fun, Dickie dear –

DICKIE. How's it all going?

GRACE. I don't know. I've been there all four days now and I've hardly understood a word that's going on. Kate says the judge is against us, but he seems a charming old gentleman to me. (*Faintly shocked.*) Sir Robert's so rude to him –

Telephone rings. GRACE answers it automatically.

Nobody in.

She rings off and turns to garden door.

(*Calling.*) Arthur! Lunch! I'll come straight down. Dickie's here. (*To DICKIE.*) Kate takes the morning session, then she comes home and relieves me with Arthur, and I go to the Court in the afternoons, so you can come with me as soon as she's in.

DICKIE. Will there be room for me?

GRACE. Oh, yes. They reserve places for the family. You never saw such crowds in all your life. And such excitement! Cheers and applause and people being turned out. It's thrilling – you'll love it, Dickie.

DICKIE. Well – if I don't understand a word –

GRACE. Oh, that doesn't matter. They all get so terribly worked up you find yourself getting worked up, too. Sir Robert and the Attorney-General go at each other hammer and tongs – you wait and hear them – all about Petitions and demurrers and prerogatives and things. Nothing to do with Ronnie at all – seems to me –

DICKIE. How did Ronnie get on in the witness box?

GRACE. Two days he was cross-examined. Two whole days. Imagine it, the poor little pet! I must say he didn't seem to mind much. He said two days with the Attorney-General wasn't nearly as bad as two minutes with Sir Robert. Kate says he made a very good impression with the jury –

DICKIE. How is Kate, Mother?

GRACE. Oh, all right. You heard about John, I suppose –

DICKIE. Yes. That's what I meant. How has she taken it?

GRACE. You can never tell with Kate. She never lets you know what she's feeling. We all think he's behaved very badly.

ARTHUR *appears at the garden door, walking very groggily.*

Arthur! You shouldn't have come up the stairs by yourself.

ARTHUR. I had little alternative.

GRACE. I'm sorry, dear. I was talking to Dickie.

GRACE *helps* ARTHUR *into the bath chair.*

ARTHUR. How are you, Dickie?

DICKIE. *(Shaking hands.)* Very well, thank you, Father.

ARTHUR. I've been forced to adopt this ludicrous form of propulsion. I apologize.

He wheels himself into the room and examines DICKIE.

You look very well. A trifle thinner, perhaps –

DICKIE. Hard work, Father.

ARTHUR. Or late hours?

DICKIE. You can't keep late hours in Reading.

ARTHUR. You could keep late hours anywhere. I've had quite a good report about you from Mr. Lamb.

DICKIE, Good egg! He's a decent old stick, the old baa-lamb. I took him racing last Saturday. Had the time of his life and lost his shirt.

ARTHUR, Did he? I have no doubt that, given the chance, you'll succeed in converting the entire Reading branch of the Westminster Bank into a bookmaking establishment. Mr. Lamb says you've joined the Territorials.

DICKIE. Yes, Father.

ARTHUR. Why have you done that?

DICKIE. Well, from all accounts there's a fair chance of a bit of a scrap quite soon. If there is I don't want it to be all over before I can get in on it –

ARTHUR. If there is what you call a scrap you'll do far better to stay in the bank –

DICKIE. Oh, no, Father. I mean, the bank's all right – but still – a chap can't help looking forward to a bit of a change – I can always go back to the bank afterwards –

The telephone rings. ARTHUR *takes receiver off and puts it down on table.*

GRACE. Oh, no, dear. You can't do that.

ARTHUR. Why not?

GRACE. It annoys the exchange.

ARTHUR. I prefer to annoy the exchange rather than have the exchange annoy me. (*To* GRACE.) Catherine's late. She was in at half-past yesterday.

GRACE. Perhaps they're taking the lunch interval later today.

ARTHUR. Lunch interval? This isn't a cricket match. (*Looking at her.*) Nor, may I say, is it a matinée at the Gaiety. Why are you wearing that highly unsuitable get-up?

GRACE. Don't you like it, dear? I think it's Mme Dupont's best.

ARTHUR. Grace – your son is facing a charge of theft and forgery –

GRACE. Oh, dear! It's so difficult! I simply can't be seen in the same old dress, day after day. (*A thought strikes her.*) I tell you what, Arthur. I'll wear my black coat and skirt tomorrow – for the verdict.

ARTHUR *glares at her, helplessly, then turns his chair to the dining-room.*

ARTHUR. Did you say my lunch was ready?

GRACE. Yes, dear. It's only cold. I did the salad myself. Violet and cook are at the trial.

DICKIE. Is Violet still with you? She was under sentence last time I saw you –

GRACE. She's been under sentence for the last six months, poor thing – only she doesn't know it. Neither your father nor I have the courage to tell her –

ARTHUR. (*Stopping at door.*) I have the courage to tell her.

GRACE. It's funny that you don't, then, dear.

ARTHUR. I will.

GRACE. (*Hastily.*) No, no, you mustn't. When it's to be done, I'll do it.

ARTHUR. You see, Dickie? These taunts of cowardice are daily flung at my head; but should I take them up I'm forbidden to move in the matter. Such is the logic of women.

He goes into the dining-room. DICKIE, *who has been holding the door open, closes it after him.*

DICKIE. (*Seriously.*) How *is* he?

GRACE *shakes her head quietly.*

Will you take him away after the trial?

GRACE. He's promised to go into a nursing home.

DICKIE. Do you think he will?

GRACE. How do I know? He'll probably find some new excuse –

DICKIE. But surely, if he loses this time, he's lost for good, hasn't he?

GRACE. (*Slowly.*) So they say, Dickie dear – I can only hope it's true.

DICKIE. How did you keep him away from the trial?

GRACE. Kate and Sir Robert together. He wouldn't listen to me or the doctor.

DICKIE. Poor old Mother! You must have been having a pretty rotten time of it, one way and another –

GRACE. I've said my say, Dickie. He knows what I think. Not that he cares. He never has – all his life. Anyway, I've given up worrying. He's always said he knew what he was doing. It's my job to try and pick up the pieces, I suppose.

CATHERINE *comes in.*

CATHERINE. Lord! The heat! Mother, can't you get rid of those reporters – Hullo, Dickie.

DICKIE. (*Embracing her.*) Hullo, Kate.

CATHERINE. Come to be in at the death.

DICKIE. Is that what it's going to be?

CATHERINE. Looks like it. I could cheerfully strangle that old brute of a judge, Mother. He's dead against us.

GRACE. (*Fixing her hat in the mirror.*) Oh, dear!

CATHERINE. Sir Robert's very worried. He said the Attorney General's speech made a great impression on the jury. I must say it was very clever. To listen to him yesterday you would have thought that a verdict for Ronnie would simultaneously cause a mutiny in the Royal Navy and triumphant jubilation in Berlin.

ARTHUR *appears in his chair, at the dining room door.*

ARTHUR. You're late, Catherine.

CATHERINE. I know, Father. I'm sorry. There was such a huge crowd outside as well as inside the Court that I couldn't get a cab. And I stayed to talk to Sir Robert.

GRACE. (*Pleased.*) Is there a bigger crowd even than yesterday, Kate?

CATHERINE. Yes, Mother. Far bigger.

ARTHUR. How did it go this morning?

CATHERINE. Sir Robert finished his cross-examination of the postmistress. I thought he'd demolished her completely. She admitted she couldn't identify Ronnie in the Commander's office. She admitted she couldn't be sure of the time he came in. She admitted that she was called away to the telephone while he was buying his fifteen-and-six postal order, and that all Osborne cadets looked alike to her in their uniforms, so that it might quite easily have been another cadet who cashed the five shillings. It was a brilliant cross-examination. So gentle and quiet. He didn't bully her, or frighten her – he just coaxed her into tying herself into knots. Then, when he'd finished the Attorney General asked her again whether she was absolutely positive that the same boy that bought the fifteen-and-six postal order also cashed the five-shilling one. She said yes. She was quite, quite sure because Ronnie was such a good-looking little boy that she had specially noticed him. She hadn't said that in her examination-in-chief. I could see those twelve good men and true nodding away to each other. I believe it undid the whole of that magnificent cross-examination.

ARTHUR. If she thought him so especially good-looking, why couldn't she identify him the same evening?

CATHERINE. Don't ask me, Father. Ask the Attorney General. I'm sure he has a beautifully reasonable answer.

DICKIE. Ronnie good-looking! What utter rot! She must be lying, that woman.

GRACE. Nonsense, Dickie! I thought he looked very well in the box yesterday, didn't you, Kate?

CATHERINE. Yes, Mother.

ARTHUR. Who else gave evidence for the other side?

CATHERINE. The Commander, the Chief Petty Officer, and one of the boys at the College.

ARTHUR. Anything very damaging?

CATHERINE. Nothing that we didn't expect. The boy showed obviously he hated Ronnie and was torn to shreds by Sir Robert. The Commander scored, though. He's an honest man and genuinely believes Ronnie did it.

GRACE. Did you see anybody interesting in Court, dear?

CATHERINE. Yes, Mother. John Watherstone.

GRACE. John? I hope you didn't speak to him, Kate.

CATHERINE. Of course I did.

GRACE. Kate, how could you! What did he say?

CATHERINE. He wished us luck.

GRACE. What impertinence! The idea of John Watherstone coming calmly up in Court to wish you luck – I think it's the most disgraceful, cold-blooded –

ARTHUR. Grace – you will be late for the resumption.

GRACE. Oh, will I? Are you ready, Dickie?

DICKIE. Yes, Mother.

GRACE. You don't think that nice, grey suit of yours you paid so much money for –

ARTHUR. What time are they resuming, Kate?

CATHERINE. Two o'clock.

ARTHUR. It's twenty past two now.

GRACE. Oh, dear! We'll be terribly late. Kate – that's your fault. Arthur, you must finish your lunch –

ARTHUR. Yes, Grace.

GRACE. Promise now.

ARTHUR. I promise.

GRACE. (*To herself.*) I wonder if Violet will remember to pick up those onions. Perhaps I'd better do it on the way back from the Court. (*As she passes* CATHERINE.) Kate, dear, I'm so sorry –

CATHERINE. What for, Mother?

GRACE. John proving such a bad hat. I never did like him very much, you know.

CATHERINE. No, I know.

GRACE. Now, Dickie, when you get to the front-door put your head down, like me, and just charge through them all.

ARTHUR. Why don't you go out by the garden?

GRACE. I wouldn't like to risk this dress getting through that hedge. Come on, Dickie. I always shout: 'I'm the maid and don't know nothing', so don't be surprised.

DICKIE. Right-oh, Mother.

GRACE *goes out.* DICKIE *follows her. There is a pause.*

ARTHUR. Are we going to lose this case, Kate?

CATHERINE *quietly shrugs her shoulders.*

It's our last chance.

CATHERINE. I know.

ARTHUR. (*With sudden violence.*) We've got to win it.

CATHERINE *does not reply.*

What does Sir Robert think?

CATHERINE. He seems very worried.

ARTHUR. (*Thoughtfully.*) I wonder if you were right, Kate. I wonder if we could have had a better man.

CATHERINE. No, Father. We couldn't have had a better man.

ARTHUR. You admit that now, do you?

CATHERINE. Only that he's the best advocate in England and for some reason – prestige, I suppose – he seems genuinely anxious to win this case. I don't go back on anything else I've ever said about him.

ARTHUR. The papers said that he began today by telling the judge he felt ill and might have to ask for an adjournment. I trust he won't collapse –

CATHERINE. He won't. It was just another of those brilliant tricks of his that he's always boasting about. It got him the sympathy of the Court and possibly – no, I won't say that –

ARTHUR. Say it.

CATHERINE. (*Slowly.*) Possibly provided him with an excuse if he's beaten.

ARTHUR. You don't like him, do you?

CATHERINE. (*Indifferently.*) There's nothing in him to like or dislike, Father. I admire him.

DESMOND *appears at the garden door. Standing inside the room, he knocks diffidently.* CATHERINE *and* ARTHUR *turn and see him.*

DESMOND. I trust you do not object to me employing this rather furtive entry. The crowds at the front-door are most alarming –

ARTHUR. Come in, Desmond. Why have you left the Court?

DESMOND. My partner will be holding the fort. He is perfectly competent, I promise you.

ARTHUR. I'm glad to hear it.

DESMOND. I wonder if I might see Catherine alone. I have a matter of some urgency to communicate to her –

ARTHUR. Oh. Do you wish to hear this urgent matter, Kate?

CATHERINE. Yes, Father.

ARTHUR. Very well. I shall go and finish my lunch.

He wheels his chair to the dining-room door. DESMOND *flies to help.*

DESMOND. Allow me.

ARTHUR. Thank you. I can manage this vehicle without assistance.

He goes out.

DESMOND. I fear I should have warned you of my visit. Perhaps I have interrupted –

CATHERINE. No, Desmond. Please sit down.

DESMOND. Thank you. I'm afraid I have only a very short time. I must get back to Court for the cross-examination of the judge-advocate.

CATHERINE. Yes, Desmond. Well?

DESMOND, I have a taxicab waiting at the end of the street.

CATHERINE. *(Smiling.)* How very extravagant of you, Desmond.

DESMOND, *(Also smiling.)* Yes. But it shows you how rushed this visit must necessarily be. The fact of the matter is – it suddenly occurred to me during the lunch recess that I had far better see you today.

CATHERINE. *(Her thoughts far distant.)* Why?

DESMOND. I have a question to put to you, Kate, which, if I had postponed putting until after the verdict, you might – who knows – have thought had been prompted by pity – if we had lost. Or – if we had won, your reply might – again who knows – have been influenced by gratitude. Do you follow me, Kate?

CATHERINE. Yes, Desmond. I think I do.

DESMOND. Ah. Then possibly you have some inkling of what the question is I have to put to you?

CATHERINE. Yes. I think I have.

DESMOND. (*A trifle disconcerted.*) Oh.

CATHERINE. I'm sorry, Desmond. I ought, I know, to have followed the usual practice in such cases, and told you I had no inkling whatever.

DESMOND. No, no. Your directness and honesty are two of the qualities I so much admire in you. I am glad you have guessed. It makes my task the easier –

CATHERINE. (*In a matter-of-fact voice.*) Will you give me a few days to think it over?

DESMOND. Of course. Of course.

CATHERINE. I need hardly tell you how grateful I am, Desmond.

DESMOND. (*A trifle bewildered.*) There is no need, Kate. No need at all –

CATHERINE *has risen brusquely.*

CATHERINE. You mustn't keep your taxi waiting –

DESMOND. Oh, bother my taxi! (*Recovering himself.*) Forgive me, Kate, but you see I know very well what your feelings for me really are.

CATHERINE. (*Gently.*) You do, Desmond?

DESMOND. Yes, Kate. I know quite well they have never amounted to much more than a sort of – well – shall we say, friendliness? A warm friendliness, I hope. Yes, I think perhaps we can definitely say, warm. But no more than that. That's true, isn't it?

CATHERINE. (*Quietly.*) Yes, Desmond.

DESMOND. I know, I know. Of course, the thing is that even if I proved the most devoted and adoring husband that ever lived – which, I may say – if you give me the chance, I intend to be – your feelings for me would never – could never – amount to more than that. When I was young it might, perhaps, have been a different story. When I played cricket for England –

He notices the faintest expression of pity that has crossed CATHERINE'S *face.*

(*Apologetically.*) And, of course, perhaps even that would not have made so much difference. Perhaps you feel I cling too much to my past athletic prowess. I feel it myself, sometimes – but the truth is I have not much else to cling to save that and my love for you. The athletic prowess is fading, I'm afraid, with the years and the stiffening of the muscles – but my love for you will never fade.

CATHERINE. (*Smiling.*) That's very charmingly said, Desmond.

DESMOND. Don't make fun of me, Kate, please. I meant it, every word. (*Clearing his throat.*) However, let's take a more mundane approach and examine the facts. Fact one: You don't love me, and never can. Fact two: I love you, always have, and always will. That is the situation – and it is a situation which, after most careful consideration, I am fully prepared to accept. I reached this decision some months ago, but thought at first it would be better to wait until this case, which is so much on all our minds, should be over. Then at lunch today I determined to anticipate the verdict tomorrow, and let you know what was in my mind at once. No matter what you feel or don't feel for me, no matter what you feel for anyone else, I want you to be my wife.

Pause.

CATHERINE. (*At length.*) I see. Thank you, Desmond. That makes everything much clearer.

DESMOND. There is much more that I had meant to say, but I shall put it in a letter.

CATHERINE. Yes, Desmond. Do.

DESMOND. Then I may expect your answer in a few days?

CATHERINE. Yes, Desmond.

DESMOND. (*Looking at his watch.*) I must get back to Court. (*He collects his hat, stick, and gloves.*) How did you think it went this morning?

CATHERINE. I thought the postmistress restored the Admiralty's case with that point about Ronnie's looks –

DESMOND. Oh, no, no. Not at all. There is still the overwhelming fact that she couldn't identify him. What a brilliant cross-examination, was it not?

CATHERINE. Brilliant.

DESMOND. He is a strange man, Sir Robert. At times, so cold and distant and – and –

CATHERINE. Fishlike.

DESMOND. Fishlike, exactly. And yet he has a real passion about this case. A real passion. I happen to know of course this must on no account go any further – but I happen to know that he has made a very, very great personal sacrifice in order to bring it to court.

CATHERINE. Sacrifice? What? Of another brief?

DESMOND. No, no. That is no sacrifice to him. No – he was offered – you really promise to keep this to yourself?

CATHERINE. My dear Desmond, whatever the Government offered him can't be as startling as all that; he's in the Opposition.

DESMOND. As it happens it was quite startling, and a most graceful compliment, if I may say so, to his performance as Attorney-General under the last Government.

CATHERINE. What was he offered, Desmond?

DESMOND. The appointment of Lord Chief Justice. He turned it down simply in order to be able to carry on with the case of Winslow versus Rex. Strange are the ways of men are they not? Goodbye, my dear.

CATHERINE. Goodbye, Desmond.

Exit DESMOND.

CATHERINE *turns from the window deep in thought. She has a puzzled, strained expression. It does not look as though it were* DESMOND *she was thinking of.* ARTHUR *opens dining-room door and peers round.*

ARTHUR. May I come in now?

CATHERINE. Yes, Father. He's gone.

ARTHUR. I'm rather tired of being gazed at from the street while eating my mutton, as though I were an animal at the Zoo.

CATHERINE. (*Slowly.*) I've been a fool, Father.

ARTHUR. Have you, my dear?

CATHERINE. An utter fool.

ARTHUR *waits for* CATHERINE *to make herself plain. She does not do so.*

ARTHUR. In default of further information, I can only repeat, have you, my dear?

CATHERINE. There can be no further information. I'm under a pledge of secrecy.

ARTHUR. Oh. What did Desmond want?

CATHERINE. To marry me.

ARTHUR. I trust the folly you were referring to wasn't your acceptance of him?

CATHERINE. (*Smiling.*) No, Father. (*She comes and sits on the arm of his chair.*) Would it be such folly, though?

ARTHUR. Lunacy.

CATHERINE. Oh, I don't know. He's nice, and he's doing very well as a solicitor.

ARTHUR. Neither very compelling reasons for marrying him.

CATHERINE. Seriously – I shall have to think it over.

ARTHUR. Think it over, by all means. But decide against it.

CATHERINE. I'm nearly thirty, you know.

ARTHUR. Thirty isn't the end of life.

CATHERINE. It might he – for an unmarried woman, with not much looks.

ARTHUR. Rubbish.

CATHERINE *shakes her head.*

Better far to live and die an old maid than to marry Desmond.

CATHERINE. Even an old maid must eat. (*Pause.*)

ARTHUR. I am leaving you and your mother everything, you know.

CATHERINE. (*Quietly.*) Everything?

ARTHUR. There is still a little left. (*Pause.*) Did you take my suggestion as regards your Suffrage Association?

CATHERINE. Yes, Father.

ARTHUR. You demanded a salary?

CATHERINE. I asked for one.

ARTHUR. And they're going to give it to you, I trust?

CATHERINE. Yes, Father. Two pounds a week.

ARTHUR. (*Angrily.*) That's insulting.

CATHERINE. No. It's generous. It's all they can afford. We're not a very rich organization – you know.

ARTHUR. You'll have to think of something else.

CATHERINE. What else? Darning socks? That's about my only other accomplishment.

ARTHUR. There must be something useful you can do.

CATHERINE. You don't think the work I am doing at the W.S.A. is useful?

ARTHUR *is silent.*

You may be right. But it's the only work I'm fitted for, all the same. (*Pause.*) No, Father. The choice is quite simple. Either I marry Desmond and settle down into quite a comfortable and not really useless existence – or I go on for the rest of my life earning two pounds a week in the service of a hopeless cause.

ARTHUR. A hopeless cause? I've never heard you say that before.

CATHERINE. I've never felt it before.

ARTHUR is silent. CATHERINE leans her head against his chair.

CATHERINE. John's going to get married next month.

ARTHUR. Did he tell you?

CATHERINE. Yes. He was very apologetic.

ARTHUR. Apologetic!

CATHERINE. He didn't need to be. It's a girl I know slightly. She'll make him a good wife.

ARTHUR. Is he in love with her?

CATHERINE. No more than he was with me. Perhaps, even, a little less.

ARTHUR. Why is he marrying her so soon after – after –

CATHERINE. After jilting me? Because he thinks there's going to be a war. If there is, his regiment will be among the first to go overseas. Besides, his father approves strongly. She's a general's daughter. Very, very suitable.

ARTHUR. Poor Kate!

Pause. He takes her hand slowly.

How I've messed up your life, haven't I?

CATHERINE. No, Father. Any messing-up that's been done has been done by me.

ARTHUR. I'm so sorry, Kate. I'm so sorry.

CATHERINE. Don't be, Father. We both knew what we were doing.

ARTHUR. Did we?

CATHERINE. I think we did.

ARTHUR. Yet our motives seem to have been different all along – yours and mine, Kate? Can we both have been right?

CATHERINE. I believe we can. I believe we have been.

ARTHUR. And yet they've always been so infernally logical, our opponents, haven't they?

CATHERINE. I'm afraid logic has never been on our side.

ARTHUR. Brute stubbornness – a selfish refusal to admit defeat. That's what your mother thinks have been our motives –

CATHERINE. Perhaps she's right. Perhaps that's all they've been.

ARTHUR. But perhaps brute stubbornness isn't such a bad quality in the face of injustice?

CATHERINE. Or in the face of tyranny. (*Pause.*) If you could go back, Father, and choose again – would your choice be different?

ARTHUR. Perhaps.

CATHERINE. I don't think so.

ARTHUR. I don't think so, either.

CATHERINE. I still say we both knew what we were doing. And we were right to do it.

ARTHUR kisses the top of her head.

ARTHUR. Dear Kate. Thank you.

There is a silence. A newsboy can be heard dimly, shouting from the street outside.

You aren't going to marry Desmond, are you?

CATHERINE. (*With a smile.*) In the words of the Prime Minister, Father – wait and see.

He squeezes her hand. The newsboy can still be heard – now a little louder.

ARTHUR. What's that boy shouting, Kate?

CATHERINE. Only – Winslow case – Latest.

ARTHUR. It didn't sound to me like 'Latest'.

CATHERINE gets up to listen at the window. Suddenly we hear it quite plainly. ' Winslow Case Result! Winslow Case Result! '

Result?

CATHERINE. There must be some mistake.

There is another sudden outburst of noise from the hall as the front door is opened. It subsides again. VIOLET comes in quickly with a broad smile.

VIOLET. Oh, sir! Oh, sir!

ARTHUR. What's happened?

VIOLET. Oh, Miss Kate, what a shame you missed it! Just after they come back from lunch, and Mrs. Winslow she wasn't there neither, nor Master Ronnie. The cheering and the shouting and the carrying-on – you never heard anything like it in all your life – and Sir Robert standing there at the table with his wig on crooked and the tears running down his face – running down his face they were, and not able to speak because of the noise. Cook and me we did a bit of crying too, we just couldn't help it – you couldn't, you know. Oh, it was lovely! We did enjoy ourselves. And then cook had her hat knocked over her eyes by the man behind who was cheering and waving his arms about something chronic, and shouting about liberty – you would have laughed, miss, to see her, she was that cross – but she didn't mind really, she was only pretending, and we kept on cheering and the judge kept on shouting, but it wasn't any good, because even the jury joined in, and some of them climbed out of the box to shake hands with Sir Robert. And then outside in the street it was just the same – you couldn't move for the crowd, and you'd think they'd all gone mad the way they were carrying on. Some of them were shouting 'Good old Winslow!' and singing 'For he's a jolly good fellow', and cook had her hat knocked off again. Oh, it was lovely! (*To* ARTHUR.) Well, sir, you must be feeling nice and pleased, now it's all over?

ARTHUR. Yes, Violet. I am.

VIOLET. That's right. I always said it would come all right in the end, didn't I?

ARTHUR. Yes. You did.

VIOLET. Two years all but one month it's been, now, since Master Ronnie come back that day. Fancy.

ARTHUR. Yes.

VIOLET. I don't mind telling you, sir, I wondered sometimes whether you and Miss Kate weren't just wasting your time carrying on the way you have all the time. Still – you couldn't have felt that if you'd been in Court today –

She turns to go and stops.

Oh, sir, Mrs. Winslow asked me to remember most particular to pick up some onions from the greengrocer, but –

CATHERINE. That's all right, Violet. I think Mrs. Winslow is picking them up herself, on her way back –

VIOLET. I see, miss. Poor Madam! What a sell for her when she gets to the Court and finds it's all over. Well, sir – congratulations, I'm sure.

ARTHUR. Thank you, Violet.

Exit VIOLET.

ARTHUR. It would appear, then, that we've won.

CATHERINE. Yes, Father, it would appear that we've won.

She breaks down and cries, her head on her father's lap.

ARTHUR. (*Slowly.*) I would have liked to have been there.

Pause.

Enter VIOLET.

VIOLET. (*Announcing.*) Sir Robert Morton!

SIR ROBERT *walks calmly and methodically into the room. He looks as spruce and neat as earlier, and* VIOLET'S *description of him in Court does not seem to tally with his composed features.*

CATHERINE *jumps up hastily and dabs her eyes.*

Exit VIOLET.

SIR ROBERT. I thought you might like to hear the actual terms of the Attorney-General's statement – (*He pulls out a scrap of paper.*) So I jotted it down for you. (*Reading.*) 'I say now, on behalf of the Admiralty, that I accept the declaration of Ronald Arthur Winslow that he did not write the name on the postal order, that he did not take it and that he did not cash it, and that consequently he was innocent of the charge which was brought against him two years ago. I make that statement without any reservation of any description, intending it to be a complete acceptance of the boy's statements.'

He folds the paper up and hands it to ARTHUR.

ARTHUR. Thank you, sir. It is rather hard for me to find the words I should speak to you.

SIR ROBERT. Pray do not trouble yourself to search for them, sir. Let us take these rather tiresome and conventional expressions of gratitude for granted, shall we? Now, on the question of damages and costs. I fear we shall find the Admiralty rather niggardly. You are likely still to be left considerably out of pocket. However, doubtless we can apply a slight spur to the First Lord's posterior in the House of Commons –

ARTHUR. Please, sir – no more trouble – I beg. Let the matter rest here. (*He shows the piece of paper.*) This is all I have ever asked for.

SIR ROBERT. (*Turning to* CATHERINE.) A pity you were not in Court, Miss Winslow. The verdict appeared to cause quite a stir.

CATHERINE. So I heard. Why did the Admiralty throw up the case?

SIR ROBERT. It was a foregone conclusion. Once the handwriting expert had been discredited – not for the first time in legal history – I knew we had a sporting chance, and no jury in the world would have convicted on the postmistress's evidence.

CATHERINE. But this morning you seemed so depressed.

SIR ROBERT. Did I? The heat in the courtroom was very trying, you know. Perhaps I was a little fatigued –

Enter VIOLET.

VIOLET. (*to* ARTHUR.) Oh, sir, the gentlemen at the front door say please will you make a statement. They say they won't go away until you do.

ARTHUR. Very well, Violet. Thank you.

VIOLET. Yes, sir.

Exit VIOLET.

ARTHUR. What shall I say?

SIR ROBERT. (*Indifferently.*) I hardly think it matters. Whatever you say will have little bearing on what they write.

ARTHUR. What shall I say, Kate?

CATHERINE. You'll think of something, Father.

She begins to wheel his chair towards the door.

ARTHUR. (*Sharply.*) No! I refuse to meet the Press in this ridiculous chariot. (*To* CATHERINE.) Get me my stick!

CATHERINE. (*Protestingly.*) Father – you know what the doctor –

ARTHUR. Get me my stick!

CATHERINE, *without more ado, gets his stick for him. She and* SIR ROBERT *help him out of his chair.*

How is this? I am happy to have lived long enough to have seen justice done to my son –

CATHERINE. It's a little gloomy, Father. You're going to live for ages yet –

ARTHUR. Am I? Wait and see. I could say: This victory is not mine. it is the people who have triumphed – as they always will triumph – over despotism. How does that strike you, sir? A trifle pretentious, perhaps.

SIR ROBERT. Perhaps, sir. I should say it, none the less. It will be very popular.

ARTHUR. Hm! Perhaps I had better say what I really feel, which is merely: Thank God we beat 'em.

He goes out. SIR ROBERT *turns abruptly to* CATHERINE.

SIR ROBERT. Miss Winslow – might I be rude enough to ask you for a little of your excellent whisky?

CATHERINE. Of course.

She goes into the dining-room. SIR ROBERT, left alone, droops his shoulders wearily. He subsides into a chair. When CATHERINE comes back with the whisky he straightens his shoulders instinctively, but does not rise.

SIR ROBERT. That is very kind. Perhaps you would forgive me not getting up? The heat in that courtroom was really so infernal.

He takes the glass from her and drains it quickly. She notices his hand is trembling slightly.

CATHERINE. Are you feeling all right, Sir Robert?

SIR ROBERT. Just a slight nervous reaction – that's all. Besides, I have not been feeling myself all day. I told the Judge so, this morning, if you remember, but I doubt if he believed me. He thought it was a trick. What suspicious minds people have, have they not?

CATHERINE. Yes.

SIR ROBERT. (*Handing her back the glass.*) Thank you.

CATHERINE puts the glass down, then turns slowly back to face him as if nerving herself for an ordeal.

CATHERINE. Sir Robert – I'm afraid I have a confession and an apology to make to you.

SIR ROBERT. (*Sensing what is coming.*) Dear lady – I am sure the one is rash and the other superfluous. I would far rather hear neither –

CATHERINE. (*With a smile.*) I am afraid you must. This is probably the last time I shall see you and it is a better penance for me to say this than to write it. I have entirely misjudged your attitude to this case, and if in doing so I have ever seemed to you either rude or ungrateful, I am sincerely and humbly sorry.

SIR ROBERT. (*Indifferently.*) My dear Miss Winslow, you have never seemed to me either rude or ungrateful. And my attitude to this case has been the same as yours – a determination to win at all costs. Only – when you talk of gratitude – you must remember that those costs were not mine, but yours.

CATHERINE. Weren't they also yours, Sir Robert?

SIR ROBERT. I beg your pardon?

CATHERINE. Haven't you too made a certain sacrifice for the case?

Pause.

SIR ROBERT. The robes of that office would not have suited me.

CATHERINE. Wouldn't they?

SIR ROBERT. (*With venom.*) And what is more, I fully intend to have Curry expelled from the Law Society.

CATHERINE. Please don't. He did me a great service by telling me —

SIR ROBERT. I must ask you never to divulge it to another living soul, and even to forget it yourself.

CATHERINE. I shall never divulge it. I'm afraid I can't promise to forget it myself.

SIR ROBERT. Very well. If you choose to endow an unimportant incident with a romantic significance, you are perfectly at liberty to do so. I must go. (*He gets up.*)

CATHERINE. Why are you always at such pains to prevent people knowing the truth about you, Sir Robert?

SIR ROBERT. Am I, indeed?

CATHERINE. You know you are. Why?

SIR ROBERT. Perhaps because *I* do not know the truth about myself.

CATHERINE. That is no answer.

SIR ROBERT. My dear Miss Winslow, are you cross-examining me?

CATHERINE. On this point, yes. Why are you so ashamed of your emotions?

SIR ROBERT. Because, as a lawyer, I must necessarily distrust them.

CATHERINE. Why?

SIR ROBERT. To fight a case on emotional grounds, Miss Winslow, is the surest way of losing it. Emotions muddy the issue. Cold, clear logic – and buckets of it – should be the lawyer's only equipment.

CATHERINE. Was it cold, clear logic that made you weep today at the verdict?

Pause.

SIR ROBERT. Your maid, of course, told you that? It doesn't matter. It will be in the papers tomorrow, anyway. (*Fiercely.*) Very well, then, if you must have it, here it is. I wept today because right had been done.

CATHERINE. Not justice?

SIR ROBERT. No. Not justice. Right. It is easy to do justice – very hard to do right. Unfortunately, while the appeal of justice is intellectual, the appeal of right appears for some odd reason to induce tears in court. That is my answer and my excuse. And now, may I leave the witness box?

CATHERINE. No. One last question. How can you reconcile your support of Winslow against the Crown with your political beliefs?

SIR ROBERT. Very easily. No one party has a monopoly of concern for individual liberty. On that issue all parties are united.

CATHERINE. I don't think so.

SIR ROBERT. You don't?

CATHERINE. No. Not all parties. Only some people from all parties.

SIR ROBERT. That is a wise remark. We can only hope, then, that those same people will always prove enough people. You would make a good advocate.

CATHERINE. Would I?

SIR ROBERT. Yes. (*Playfully.*) Why do you not canalize your feministic impulses towards the law courts, Miss Winslow, and abandon the lost cause of women's suffrage?

CATHERINE, Because I don't believe it *is* a lost cause.

SIR ROBERT. No? Are you going to continue to pursue it?

CATHERINE. Certainly.

SIR ROBERT. You will be wasting your time.

CATHERINE. I don't think so.

SIR ROBERT. A pity. In the House of Commons in days to come I shall make a point of looking up at the Gallery in the hope of catching a glimpse of you in that provocative hat.

RONNIE *comes in. He is fifteen now, and there are distinct signs of an incipient man-about-town. He is very smartly dressed in a lounge suit and homburg hat.*

RONNIE. I say, Sir Robert, I'm most awfully sorry. I didn't know anything was going to happen.

SIR ROBERT. Where were you?

RONNIE. At the pictures.

SIR ROBERT. Pictures? What is that?

CATHERINE. Cinematograph show.

RONNIE. I'm most awfully sorry. I say – we won, didn't we?

SIR ROBERT. Yes. We won. Goodbye, Miss Winslow. Shall I see you in the House then, one day?

CATHERINE. (*With a smile.*) Yes, Sir Robert. One day. But not in the Gallery. Across the floor.

SIR ROBERT. (*With a faint smile.*) Perhaps. Goodbye. (*He turns to go.*)

Curtain.